PEW SISTERS

Real women.
Real lives.
Real stories of God's faithfulness.

A Women's Small-Group Bible Study
✴ **Katie Schuermann** ✴

CONCORDIA PUBLISHING HOUSE • SAINT LOUIS

For my favorite pew sister,
CYNTHIA ROLEY

Published by Concordia Publishing House
3558 S. Jefferson Avenue, St. Louis, MO 63118-3968
1-800-325-3040 · www.cph.org

Manufactured in the United States of America

6 7 8 9 10   22 21 20 19 18 17

TABLE OF CONTENTS

FOREWORD

Is it important to have devotion books and Bible studies written by women for women? Or is this a fruit of feminism that we would be fine without?

I enjoy many devotions written by men. Luther, Giertz, and Starck come to mind. All have provided the Church with wonderful books, none of which have made me feel misunderstood as a female. Why, then, the push for gender specific material?

The curses issued to Adam and Eve in the garden were not the same. They were as unique as the creatures themselves: "male and female He created them" (Genesis 1:27). As one's identity and essence are understood according to one's sex, so are one's sufferings and crosses. Why should there not exist a line of women's resources?

The problem is that many women's resources fail to meet a mark of excellence. One who considers what women's devotion to read is wise to proceed with discernment and frame her decision based on a few evaluative marks.

First, is the book anti-male? Does the author have an insensitive jerk of a man hiding in the shadows of her words? If so, this book should not be promoted in the Church. Even light jokes and bantering made at men's expense often prove more harmful than humorous. Degrading males to promote females does not edify the Body of Christ.

Second, does the book reduce women to a pile of clichés? Ultimately: is it anti-female? Too many resources aimed at women are content to take up topics amounting to a shallow definition of womanhood. Women like chocolate! Women like shoes! Women like jewelry! Women like spas! These are all true of me and I feel no shame in admitting it. But while I like them, I do not define myself according to them. I would like my devotional resource to provide a level of gravity that reflects not just my interests but also my essence—who I am as a human being in general and a woman in particular.

Finally, is the book theologically sound and doctrinally rich? Or is it vacuous or heterodox? If women are liberated enough to roar, surely we are strong enough to insist on faithful interpretation and application of Scripture.

Pew Sisters meets all of these expectations. It is in no way disrespectful to men. It never suggests that women have to care for other women because pastors or husbands or fathers or brothers are failing in this sphere.

Pew Sisters recognizes a depth to femininity. Where other resources have disappointed me with superficialities and trivialities, this book addresses heart-wrenching realities of womanhood with compassion and seriousness. Postpartum depression, broken hearts, and cancer are a few of the topics taken up in this book. All are real issues of substance paired with real stories of God's faithfulness.

As for its theological integrity, the author rightly understands her role. She understands that she is a member of the priesthood of the baptized, and is therefore charged with the proper handling of God's Word. She shares Scripture in a way that is faithful and true. She also understands that she is not a called and ordained servant of the Word. She does not edge out the role of pastors in the care of women. She wisely solicits responses from two exceptional pastors in her study guide. She puts her readers on the receiving end of correct teaching and faithful Gospel proclamation.

Pew Sisters is a women's Bible study resource that deserves a place of honor on my bookshelf and yours. Where other women's books have failed, Katie Schuermann's does not. In each session, she carries a woman in pain through a terrible trial. Her focus is on the cross of Christ, the source of genuine comfort. In telling the stories of twelve women, she bears their burdens, as all of us are called to do. She makes no distinction based on the type of trial that a woman endures. She imposes no demographical limitations. She knows that age, personality, and background are unimportant because Katie recognizes something about *true* sisterhood.

Sisterhood can be defined broadly by a pair of common chromosomes. In a circle of friends, it may have something to do with similar interests or outlook on life. In a family, a sister might be one who shares a set of childhood memories. But in the Church, true sisterhood—pew sisterhood—is this: loving one another for the sake of the eternal ties that are ours through Baptism and the Lord's Supper. This is why we rejoice with those who rejoice and mourn with those who mourn.

In my church, I teach the young women's high school Sunday School class. I may not shop at American Eagle or read the *Twilight* series, and a thirty-one-year-old woman may seem quite old to them, but we are sisters in Christ's name. I also attend a women's Bible study where the average age is sixty-five. I don't possess their level of wisdom, and a thirty-one-year-old woman may seem quite young to them, but we are sisters in Christ's name. All of us, regardless of background or age, are privileged and blessed to be listening ears and crying shoulders for one another. Katie's book encourages us to true Christian sisterhood, out of love for our neighbor and in gratitude for Christ's great love for us.

By Rose E. Adle

HOW TO USE THIS BOOK

Every woman sitting in the pew has a story to share of God's faithfulness in her life, and we women love nothing more than to revel in one another's experiences and celebrate the sisterhood of believers. *Pew Sisters* helps get that celebration started. Devotional in both tone and form, this twelve-session study goes and tells what God has done in the lives of real women in the Church today. From alcoholism to postpartum depression to cancer, women from all over the Church generously share their stories for the consolation and encouragement of their fellow sisters in Christ.

Each session begins with a Scripture reading followed by a narrative of an individual woman's real-life story. Eight study questions, designed for both personal and group study, help the reader apply the reading and narrative to her own life in Christ. "A Moment in the Pew," a segment designed specifically for this book, offers direct suggestions for how the reader can care for the needs of her fellow pew sisters. A meditative hymn stanza and collect complete each session.

This book was written by a woman for women, but it is not intended to supplant proper pastoral care. Your pastor is Christ's man there for you, and his job is to preach and teach God's Word to you in its truth and purity. Engage your pastor in a discussion about this book. Ask him the questions at the end of each session, and listen to his answers. That's what I did. I asked my own pastors, Rev.

Brent McGuire and Rev. Michael Schuermann, every one of these questions and then compiled their answers in a study guide at the end of this book. What Gospel words of comfort they spoke to me, and what a privilege it is to share their words in this book for your benefit!

I hope your faith is strengthened, your soul comforted, and your joy multiplied in reading this book. I couldn't help but write it. There are so many of you out there whom I love and admire. Your stories must be shared, your tales must be told, and the songs of God's faithfulness to all of us in Christ Jesus must be sung. Who am I to keep these treasures to myself? Soli Deo gloria.

SUGGESTIONS FOR SMALL-GROUP PARTICIPANTS

1. Begin small-group time with prayer.

2. Every participant should feel free to express her thoughts. Comments shared in the small group should remain confidential unless you have received permission to share them outside your group.

3. If your meeting time does not allow you to discuss all of the questions for the study session, the leader should choose the questions most meaningful to the group.

4. Close by sharing concerns and prayer requests, then praying together.

INTRODUCTION

My husband and I have moved eight times in our ten years of marriage. From graduate school in Missouri to career advancements in Illinois to seminary in Indiana to my husband's first call to serve a congregation in Texas, we have set ourselves down on a lot of different pews in a lot of different churches. No matter the location, I always find myself sitting next to the most amazing sisters in Christ.

There was Diana in Kansas City. A woman with the most beautiful smile, striking figure, and gentle demeanor, she never married. She was just one year shy of retiring as an executive with AT&T, and she hoped to move back to her family's pecan farm in Oklahoma to make and sell chocolate truffles in their storefront. I remember that she used to open her hymnal before each service and let the wise words of hope and comfort written there preach a rhyming sermon to her every Sunday. I wonder if Diana ever found the perfect truffle recipe.

Then, there was Margie in Illinois. A woman in her sixties with boundless energy, she could rollerblade and bike me into oblivion. I used to love sitting at her breakfast bar, eating apples with peanut butter, talking about life, family, and faith. She and her husband generously opened their home to us when we were house-less the month before we moved to seminary. I am pretty sure Margie can still bench press more than me today.

In a country church in northern Indiana, I sat next to a tall, stately woman with broad shoulders and long eyelashes. She was never without company in church. Her children, grandchildren, and great grandchildren happily gathered around her before and after each service, but she made a point to sit next to me. I had no children, and my husband was busy serving up front as a field worker. I think she didn't want me to feel alone. Sadly, I can't remember that regal woman's name, but I will never forget her kindness.

In Texas, I sat next to Elvina. She was so slight of frame, a strong breeze could have lifted her off the ground; however, her spirit was strong and steady. She had trouble gathering enough air into her lungs to speak full sentences, but her bright eyes spoke volumes of the ninety years she had already lived on this earth. Almost single-handedly, she organized and built a deaf ministry in our church, and she persisted in climbing the sanctuary steps every Christmas and Easter to water the poinsettias and lilies. Never mind her walker. I won't soon forget the way my dear friend rested her tired head against my shoulder as I sang the Offertory to her just days before she died.

These beautiful women are my pew sisters, and, since we are all one in the Body of Christ, they are your pew sisters too. They are your family. They share the same faith as you, eat at the same table as you, and inherit the same paradise as you. Their joys are your joys, and their sorrows are your sorrows. So, please welcome them in the pages ahead. Don't be too concerned with their age or experience. Don't worry about their marital status, their education, or their waist size. Don't be bothered with whether or not they have anything in common with you, for the only thing that matters—the only thing you need to know—is that all of them have been baptized into the same Christ as you, and you are one in Him.

Session One

MARIANNE

Therefore, since we have been justified by faith, we have peace with God through our Lord Jesus Christ. Through Him we have also obtained access by faith into this grace in which we stand, and we rejoice in hope of the glory of God. Not only that, but we rejoice in our sufferings, knowing that suffering produces endurance, and endurance produces character, and character produces hope, and hope does not put us to shame, because God's love has been poured into our hearts through the Holy Spirit who has been given to us. For while we were still weak, at the right time Christ died for the ungodly. For one will scarcely die for a righteous person—though perhaps for a good person one would dare even to die—but God shows His love for us in that while we were still sinners, Christ died for us. Romans 5:1–8

We are as sick as our secrets.

Marianne grew up in a small town in Indiana. She was baptized at a Lutheran church in nearby Bloomington, but her parents were not all that interested in making the drive to church every Sunday. Marianne's grandmother, a faithful churchgoer, saw to it that her granddaughter got involved with the local Methodist congregation.

Marianne loved church. She liked the closeness of the relationships she formed there, the special attention she received from her beloved pastor's wife, and the feeling of being a part of something bigger than herself. She felt safe and secure at church, totally loved and accepted by God, and she never wanted to be apart from it.

Several years later, Marianne stood at the back of her treasured church and turned to speak to her father. "I don't want to go down the aisle," she confessed. Clark, her high school sweetheart, was waiting for her there. Marianne knew deep down inside that Clark was a spoiled child, but his good social standing suited her family and friends. Whatever her fears, it was easier for Marianne to go through with the wedding than to disappoint the people she loved.

Life was not so bad in the early years of their marriage. In fact, it was good. Clark and Marianne were blessed with the birth of two boys, and their little family moved to Bloomington where Clark got a job as a television director. Marianne could hardly contain her excitement to be back at the church where she had been baptized. She delighted in the majesty of the church's Gothic architecture, and she fell in love with the Scripture-rich liturgy of the service. Clark even came to church with her and the boys, and the two soon got involved in a couples' club. Their entire social life revolved completely around the church. This was the life for which Marianne had always dreamed.

Unfortunately, dreams have a way of ending with the dawning of a new day. Before long, Clark got a different job in Nashville, and he moved the family to Tennessee. Part of Clark's new position was wining and dining country western stars, so he began drinking. It was social drinking, at first, even sophisticated, just a part of the job. Within a few years, however, the drinking had become more personal than social. He moved the family to Georgia for yet another job change, and all kinds of things went wrong at once. The worst of it was when both of Clark's parents died, and his drinking got out of control.

"Alcoholics are all yellow lights. No reds," Marianne admitted years later to a close friend. "They keep accelerating when they should be braking."

Clark began spending large amounts of money on booze, and it soon became hard to pay the bills. Marianne feared the sight of the mailman and the sound of the telephone for all of the bad news they brought her. She knew they were living a lie, but she worked tirelessly to keep up a good front. She was terrified of anyone finding out the truth.

Church no longer felt like a blessed sanctuary from the world, for Clark brought his pungent secrets into the pews. Marianne would seethe as she sat next to him, hating him for smelling like alcohol, hating him for behaving poorly to their friends, and hating him for being a hypocrite to their boys. Clark insisted on continuing to serve as Kevin and Joe's scout leader even as he was drinking the family into debt. Marianne realized she could no longer trust the man she married, and she fumed in the jail cell of her duplicitous life.

One by one, Marianne lost control of everything she valued: her marriage, her family, her social life, her financial stability, even herself. She was sick from their secrets, and she became nasty and vindictive. One day, after a particularly bitter fight, Clark sought refuge on the backyard patio with a beer. As soon as Marianne heard the tab go up on the can, she went outside, picked up the beer, and poured its contents all over her husband. Clark wasted no time in his vengeance. He went inside the house, cleaned himself up, put on his nicest clothes, and walked out the door to meet up with another woman. He never came back.

Marianne was a wreck; her broken marriage run aground and her life's goals lost at sea. How did this happen? How did a small-town girl from Indiana become a single mother in Atlanta? How would she care for her boys? She had been a stay-at-home mom all of these years, so who would ever hire her? Marianne looked in the mirror and said to herself, "I hate you. I really do."

Marianne had to sell the house and move the boys into an apartment. She cried all of the time. One day, she came home to find that her boys had made her a coupon book, and each coupon read, "Good for one free cry." Marianne clung to her boys, feeling for the first time in what seemed like years the total love and acceptance she had cherished from her childhood days. It was a tiny flicker of hope in an otherwise bleak existence. She knew something needed to change, but she felt so helpless and alone. "Lord," she cried out, "if You want me to change, then You are going to have to do it. I just can't."

Marianne's pastor began to look in on her and the boys. He even helped them with money. Soon, Marianne was sharing her story with him, unveiling her secrets and confessing her bitter anger. In return, her pastor shared with her the complete love and acceptance of Christ. Could Jesus really love her when she felt so unlovable? Could Jesus really forgive her of her anger and hate when she still felt so angry?

Marianne pondered these divine mysteries as she attended meetings for Al-Anon, a support group for friends and families of problem drinkers. The other members talked of complete love and acceptance as well, not just for themselves but for those who had hurt them the most. "I learned today that I have to forgive the other people in my life," one woman spoke with quiet authority. "I don't have to like my husband, but I do have to love him and let my resentments go. It helps if I pray for him every day: 'Lord, I forgive him. Help me to forgive him!'" Marianne was stunned by the idea. *Forgive Clark?* Was it possible to forgive the one who had rejected and abandoned her?

One evening, Marianne sat in her car, waiting in the church parking lot for Kevin and Joe to finish their scout meeting. She sat in the darkness, wrestling with the equation of forgiveness. She thought back to her pastor's promise that Christ completely loved and accepted her, faults and all. The seed of the Word which her pastor had planted in her heart was blossoming into a tender flower of faith, and the simple truth of God's mercy to her in Jesus rang out loud and clear in the car as if God was speaking directly to her: "I have loved you all along, My child, and you are okay."

The shackles of Marianne's secrets burst open and lay in a defeated pile at her feet. Oh, the sweet freedom! The blessed joy and peace which surpasses all understanding!

But, what about Clark? How would she forgive him?

That flower of faith grew a little taller, and Marianne smiled in her understanding. "Yes," she whispered aloud to the One who is always listening, "I can forgive Clark because You have forgiven me of everything."

And, she did.

STUDY QUESTIONS

1. What in your life makes you feel unlovable?

2. Is God's love based on our worthiness?

3. How does God show us His love?

4. Does God ever withhold His love from us,
   His baptized children?

5. How does forgiveness relate to love?

----

6. Is forgiveness a feeling?

----

7. Marianne felt unworthy of God's forgiveness, yet
   God still forgives her. How can we trust that God
   forgives us of our sins even though we are unworthy?

----

8. How do we forgive those who have hurt us the most?

A MOMENT IN THE PEW

Forgiveness is not a feeling. It is a gift that is given to you regardless of how you feel. It is just as real and certain and valid whether you feel sad, happy, stressed, peaceful, guilty, or content. How do we know this to be true? God's Word tells us that forgiveness is His work for us in Christ Jesus. Forgiveness was earned for us once and for all when Jesus died on the cross to atone for our sins. It is an outpouring of God's love for us, and it is our faith, not our feelings, which grasps onto this forgiveness.

For this reason, we can forgive our sister in Christ even when we feel angry and forsaken. We can pray along with Marianne, "I forgive her. Help me to forgive her." Believe that God can forgive all sins, even yours, and forgive your pew sister for Christ's sake. When, in the inevitable moment that Satan reignites the fire of anger toward your sister in Christ, snuff it out with God's Word and ask God to help you trust in His objective promises, not in your subjective feelings. Then, tell Satan to go to hell.

HYMN STANZAS FOR MEDITATION

Lord of All Nations, Grant Me Grace
    Forgive me, Lord, where I have erred
    By loveless act and thoughtless word.
    Make me to see the wrong I do
    Will grieve my wounded Lord anew.

    Give me Thy courage, Lord, to speak
    Whenever strong oppress the weak.
    Should I myself the victim be,
    Help me forgive, rememb'ring Thee.
    (*LSB* 844:3, 4)

Collect

Heavenly Father, we act horribly and abandon You in
our thoughts, words, and deeds, yet You forgive us.
Send us Your Holy Spirit that we might grasp Your
mercy in repentance and faith and, being forgiven
of all, help us to forgive those who sin against us,
through Jesus Christ, Your Son, our Lord, who died for
all of our sin. Amen.

CLAIRE

Have you not known? Have you not heard? The Lord is the everlasting God, the Creator of the ends of the earth. He does not faint or grow weary; His understanding is unsearchable. He gives power to the faint, and to him who has no might He increases strength. Even youths shall faint and be weary, and young men shall fall exhausted; but they who wait for the Lord shall renew their strength; they shall mount up with wings like eagles; they shall run and not be weary; they shall walk and not faint. Isaiah 40:28–31

Claire sat listlessly on her living room couch. She could hear Lydia crying again in the nursery, but Claire did not move. Lydia probably wanted to nurse again. It seemed that all Lydia ever wanted to do was nurse. Or cry. Why wouldn't she ever sleep?

Claire's mother-in-law came in from the kitchen and set a fruit smoothie down on the coffee table. "I made this for you. I think it'll help you feel better. You need to keep up your strength. Breast-feeding can take a lot out of a woman." She eyed Claire with concern. Not even a week had gone by since the birth and Claire had already lost of all her baby weight. "Stay here and drink. I'll go check on Lydia."

Claire stared uninterested at the smoothie. She reached, instead, for the laundry basket on the floor. Maybe she could finally finish folding this load from yesterday. She winced in pain as she bent over to grab a green towel. When would all of the agonizing aches and stabs and stings and throbs stop? Twenty hours of labor was difficult enough, but no one warned her how long it would take for her body to heal after the trauma of birth.

Claire's mother-in-law came back into the living room with a fussy Lydia. "I think she's hungry."

Really? Claire did not know whether to scream in frustration or to cry from despair. All she wanted was to be able to fold the laundry uninterrupted, just once. Was that really too much to ask? Claire dropped the towel back into the basket and reached for Lydia. She stared at her baby girl and tried to muster up some kind of motherly affection toward the writhing bundle, but nothing came. Claire felt completely detached. What was wrong with her?

"She's so pretty, isn't she?" Claire's mother-in-law crooned.

Claire looked down at the suckling child and saw only one thing: a parasite. Yes, a little parasite that was slowly sucking the life out of her.

It had not started out this way. Claire and Todd had been so happy at first to find out they were pregnant. They had even surprised Claire's parents with the pregnancy news on her dad's fiftieth birthday. All of them had celebrated the pending arrival of the first grandchild in the family. Yet, even then, Claire could remember having trouble breathing, a definite feeling of being stifled.

"I can't seem to take a deep, cleansing breath," Claire had mentioned to Todd one day during the pregnancy. They had both shrugged it off at the time, assuming it was probably just the growing baby pushing against Claire's internal organs. Neither of them gave thought to the fact that it might be an indication of stress, that Claire might be suppressing some feelings of anxiety and fear. In fact, Claire never once allowed herself during her pregnancy to consider the enormity of how life was going to change once the baby came.

Now, Claire felt the magnitude of life's change full force. "I just don't think I can do it anymore," she wept to Todd later that night.

Todd looked at his wife; her emaciated frame, the dark circles under her eyes, the despair. He was worried. "Let me take care of Lydia for a little while so that you can go for a walk and get some fresh air. A little time by yourself will probably help you feel better."

Claire's heart jumped at the thought of having a moment all to herself, but she immediately felt a stab of guilt for wanting to be away from her own child. She turned her eyes away from Todd and shook her head no.

Weeks went by, and Claire sank into a deeper darkness. She felt trapped by her circumstances. She did not know how to fix the problems in her life or how to make them better. Why did Lydia cry instead of sleep? Why did she and Todd have to get pregnant on their honeymoon? Why couldn't she get to have a couple of years with her husband before having the responsibility of caring for Lydia? What about her own career goals? Claire felt stripped of all power and control in her life, and she fell to her knees in utter hopelessness.

"Why, God, have You abandoned me to a joyless life?" she cried out.

Yet, even as the devil tried to drown Claire in the ocean of postpartum depression, one truth kept her afloat: "I am

Christ's. I have His name written upon my heart. I am a baptized child of God, and the devil cannot have me." In the darkness of her thoughts, that simple truth became a lighthouse for Claire, a spot of peace and safety in the storm of her life. She fixed her eyes on Jesus, trusting in His promise to preserve and sustain her even as her ship threatened to overturn from the waves.

It was then that God threw Claire a lifeline and pulled her back to the safety of dry land. Todd soon made a career change that required the family to move to a different state. Forced to live away from their family, Claire found herself caring for Lydia all by herself. Even in her depression, Claire knew that some structure was needed for both her and Lydia to be at their best, so she decided to enforce a sleeping schedule for her baby. At first it was difficult to weather the crying, but Lydia soon adjusted and began sleeping through the night. Claire began sleeping through the night too.

Empowered by the success, Claire began experimenting with her own diet, eventually discovering that Lydia was lactose intolerant. The change in Claire's eating habits resulted in a happier Lydia and a calmer mommy. Claire was surprised to find herself beginning to enjoy time spent with her daughter, even time spent nursing.

During one of Lydia's feedings, Claire stared openly at her daughter's face. No doubt about it, Lydia had her mommy's forehead and her daddy's eyes. Who will this child grow up to be? What will be her favorite book? Who will she love? Claire was hooked, line and sinker, by her little girl, and she was deeply moved to realize that her dreams for the future were now intricately woven with the thread of Lydia.

Just a few short months before, Claire had despised her role as a mother. She had felt that God was somehow stripping her of all independence and power in life when, in fact, He was actually empowering her to better serve her neighbor. God gave Claire the special talents of organization, discipline, and endurance that would be needed to carry out the good work of caring for Lydia. Now, not only does Claire enjoy her vocation as a mother, but she is really good at it.

Claire still remembers the darkness, but she does not live in fear of it. In Christ, she survived it, and she will continue to survive it, come what may, even unto eternal life.

STUDY QUESTIONS

1. What darkness threatens to overpower your own life?

2. Claire struggled for months against the darkness of postpartum depression, yet she waited on the Lord. What does it mean to wait on the Lord?

3. What does God promise for those who wait on Him? (Isaiah 40:31)

4. Satan is our adversary, and he prowls around like a roaring lion seeking whom he may devour. As baptized Christians, does the devil have any power over us?

5. What is our greatest resistance against the devil? (Ephesians 6:10–18)

6. Consider the text of stanza 3 of Luther's hymn, "A Mighty Fortress Is Our God" (*LSB* 656):

> Though devils all the world should fill,
> All eager to devour us,
> We tremble not, we fear no ill;
> They shall not overpow'r us.
> This world's prince may still
> Scowl fierce as he will,
> He can harm us none.
> He's judged; the deed is done;
> On little word can fell him.

What word is it that can fell the devil?

7. Our sinful flesh fails us in this world, and we often suffer from ailments such as depression. What does God promise us amidst our suffering? (Romans 8:18–28)

8. In light of God's promises, how was Claire's postpartum depression a blessing?

A MOMENT IN THE PEW

One out of every four women will experience depression at one point in her life.[1] Depression is a legitimate, physiological, clinically diagnosed illness, and it can burden even the most devout of Christians. Its occurrence does not serve to indicate whether or not someone's faith is weak, for a baptized Christian can believe in the Good News of Jesus's saving work and still be depressed. Stress, exhaustion, anxiety, shame, and other depressive symptoms can plague even those who trust in God's grace and mercy.

How can we help our sisters in Christ who suffer from depression? God's Word tells us that Christ's strength is made perfect in our weakness, so we, as sisters in Christ, are in a prime position to remind each other of God's promise to be faithful to us even through our illnesses. Encourage your suffering sister in Christ to be in church every Sunday where she can receive Christ's gifts of Word and Sacrament to strengthen her through her trials, help her to seek the proper medical and pharmacological support she requires, and faithfully connect her to your heavenly Father in prayer.

1. Dr. Beverly K. Yahnke's introduction to *I Trust When Dark My Road*, p. 6.

God's Own Child, I Gladly Say It
>Satan, hear this proclamation:
>>I am baptized into Christ!
>Drop your ugly accusation,
>>I am not so soon enticed.
>Now that to the font I've traveled,
>All your might has come unraveled,
>And, against your tyranny,
>God, my Lord, unites with me! (*LSB* 594:3)

Collect

Victorious Lord, You conquered sin, death, and the devil on the cross. They no longer have dominion over us, Your baptized children. Grant us faith which trusts in Your victory, waits patiently on You, and endures unto life everlasting. In Jesus' name. Amen.

Session Three

JULIA

"Therefore I tell you, do not be anxious about your life, what you will eat or what you will drink, nor about your body, what you will put on. Is not life more than food, and the body more than clothing? Look at the birds of the air: they neither sow nor reap nor gather into barns, and yet your heavenly Father feeds them. Are you not of more value than they? And which of you by being anxious can add a single hour to his span of life? And why are you anxious about clothing? Consider the lilies of the field, how they grow: they neither toil nor spin, yet I tell you, even Solomon in all his glory was not arrayed like one of these. But if God so clothes the grass of the field, which today is alive and tomorrow is thrown into the oven, will He not much more clothe you, O you of little faith? Therefore do not be anxious, saying, 'What shall we eat?' or 'What shall we drink?' or 'What shall we wear?' For the Gentiles seek after all these things, and your heavenly Father knows that you need them all. But seek first the kingdom of God and His righteousness, and all these things will be added to you. Therefore do not be anxious about tomorrow, for tomorrow will be anxious for itself. Sufficient for the day is its own trouble." Matthew 6:25–34

"Julia, get up," Michael gently shook his wife awake. "They're predicting that Katrina's going to hit us head on."

Julia sat up in bed, suddenly alert. "How soon?"

"She's still a couple days out, but we need to get ready."

Michael and Julia hurriedly began the preparations.

"Grab anything that can blow away," Michael instructed their two sons. Kyle and Sam carried lawn furniture and potted plants into the house while Michael secured objects outside that could possibly become projectiles in the wind. Flying debris was always a danger in hurricanes, and the last thing they needed was a wind chime to come crashing through one of their windows.

"Do you think we should evacuate?" Michael asked as he came back into the house.

Julia nodded yes. She was not afraid of flood waters, but she didn't want to risk endangering the boys. "We could go to my parents in Fairhope," she suggested.

"That's still the Central Gulf Coast. What if the storm turns and hits them?"

"At least we'll be on high ground," Julia pointed out. "Anything is better than staying in this bowl."

Michael agreed. They quickly loaded the kids, three dogs, two kittens, one boa constrictor, and nine guinea pigs into the car. "Really?" Michael asked, nodding his head at the guinea pigs.

"They're Shawna's," Julia explained. "She can't evacuate because of her job at the hospital, so she asked if we could take them."

"We'll be a regular Noah's ark."

Julia kissed her tolerant husband's cheek and went inside

the house for one last perusal. She spied a file folder of papers sitting on the corner of her dresser and, as an afterthought, grabbed it on her way out the door.

Michael, Julia, the boys, and all of the animals waited out the storm at Julia's parents' house on the coast of Alabama. Even there, Hurricane Katrina's destructive arm tore down tree limbs, knocked debris against the house, and struck down electrical lines.

"If it's this bad here," Julia wondered, "how bad is it at home?"

The next day, the whole family watched in horror as the television set revealed blood-chilling images of a flooded, wrecked New Orleans.

"Even if the house is still there, we won't be able to get to it any time soon," Julia reasoned. "The roads are flooded, gas lines have been shut down, and our phones are gridlocked. What are we going to do?"

"We might have to start from scratch," Michael said. He logged onto the internet and checked his employer's Web site. "My company just put up a notice. They are offering temporary employment for all New Orleans employees at dealerships in both San Antonio and Dallas."

"I have a third cousin in Fort Worth," Julia offered.

"Then, Dallas it is," Michael confirmed, quickly adding, "at least for a few months."

Michael, Julia, and the boys loaded up the car once again and drove straight through to Dallas. Michael's company immediately set him up with a sales job at a Lexus dealership, and the Federal Emergency Management Administration provided a hotel room for the family. The next step was to get the boys back in school. Kyle and Sam had only completed one week of classes in New Orleans before needing to evacuate.

"Hey, there's a Lutheran high school in Dallas," Michael announced, his finger holding a place in the *L*s in the hotel room phone book. Julie picked up the phone and called the number immediately.

"You are here from New Orleans?" the woman on the other end of the line asked. "Lord, have mercy! And you have a son who is a freshman in high school? Where are you, right now? If you can get here, we'll take care of your son."

The whole family toured the high school that same morning. The woman who showed them around also saw to it that Kyle was given some school clothes. It was a good thing, for all he had with him were swim trunks, flip-flops, and beach clothes.

"How old is your brother?" the woman asked Kyle, eyeing Sam.

"He's in fifth grade."

"Is that so?" the woman smiled, clearly delighted. "Well, what do you know? My husband happens to be a fifth grade teacher at a Lutheran grade school not far from here. Sam will love it there!"

Julia retrieved the file folder she had grabbed off her bedroom dresser and waved it excitedly at Michael. The folder contained the boys' school records—report cards, birth certificates, immunization records, all of it—and they would be able to enroll the boys in school that very day. Less than twenty-four hours had passed since they pulled into Dallas, and already God was completely providing for their needs.

The provisions kept coming. Later that evening, as they stood in a grocery store parking lot, a floral shop owner overheard Julia and Michael talking.

"You are Katrina victims?" he asked. He gallantly handed Julia a rose and insisted on giving Michael a flat screen television from his own home. "Please, take it. It'll help the boys."

The next morning, Michael picked up the family in a Lexus borrowed from the dealership. "They insisted I use it," he said. "They didn't think we could manage the daily school carpool with just one car."

Michael and Julia dropped Kyle off at the high school and then walked Sam into his new classroom at the grade school. The sight of Sam's desk made them stop in their tracks. It was piled high with books, markers, pencils, school supplies, and gift certificates for shoes and school uniforms. Someone had even paid for two months worth of school lunches for Sam. Julia started crying, overwhelmed by the generosity of the church and school families.

Over the next few days, another school mother helped Julia and Michael find a temporary apartment and connected them with a local volunteer mission office that was hosting a furniture drive for Katrina victims. The mission provided them with bed frames, mattresses, two chests of drawers, a kitchen table with chairs, a love seat, and three laundry baskets full of bathroom, kitchen, and bedroom necessities.

"I think God wants us in Dallas," Sam announced to his family over dinner one night.

"Well, you'll have to talk to Daddy about that," Julia said, carefully eyeing her husband. "His company wants him back in New Orleans when things settle down."

"I think we should stay here too," Kyle announced. "I really like my school."

Michael stared thoughtfully at his plate. "I guess I could inquire about permanent positions here in Dallas."

The next day, Michael came home with a grin on his face. "I guess we had better start looking for a house."

"Why's that?" Julia asked.

"Because they offered me a full-time job!"

Sam cheered out loud. "See? I told you God wants us to stay in Dallas!"

Later that night, Michael and Julia discussed the matter in earnest.

"It wouldn't be too hard to relocate here," Michael said. "Our house in New Orleans was just a rental, and the land we were hoping to purchase and build on is now nine feet under water. We have no financial ties to anything."

"And I have a friend back home whose apartment flooded and needs a place to stay," Julia added. "If we stay here, she could take the rental house."

Michael nodded. "We could go back to New Orleans over Thanksgiving break and get the rest of our stuff."

"I don't think we'll even need most of it," Julia said. "We've been given most of what we need here in Dallas. We can leave what we don't need in New Orleans for people who lost their homes."

Michael grinned. "Speaking of homes, I haven't had a chance to tell you yet. Do you remember Kara, my brother-in-law's sister?"

Julia nodded.

"Well, she and her husband have a house to sell in Dallas, and they'll let us rent it until we are ready to buy."

Julia felt tears of gratefulness filling her eyes. The new job, the furniture, the car, the supportive schools, the television, and now a new home. Clearly, God was providing for their every need. He would continue to faithfully care for them wherever they lived. Julia was sure of it.

"Well," she laughed through her tears, "who gets to tell Sam the good news?"

STUDY QUESTIONS

1. We have all heard the old adage: "God helps those who helps themselves." Does this saying hold up in light of God's Word? (Matthew 6:25–34)

2. Is God's help dependent on our own thought, word, or deed?

3. Does God help only the righteous?

4. Does worrying do us any good?

_____

_____

_____

_____

_____

5. How do we cast our anxieties on the Lord?
   (1 Peter 5:7)

_____

_____

_____

_____

_____

6. What does it mean to "seek first the kingdom of God
   and His righteousness" (Matthew 6:33)?

_____

_____

_____

_____

_____

7. How can we know with assurance that God will,
   indeed, provide for our every need?

_____

_____

8. God faithfully guided Julia and her family to the things they needed. Can you think of a time in your life when God guided you to the things you needed?

A MOMENT IN THE PEW

od provided for Julia and her family through various people and organizations: family, friends, churches, schools, government, and even strangers. You have the means to help people in your own church and community. You can share your time with others by mentoring underprivileged children in your neighborhood or taking care of an elderly neighbor's yard; you can share your talents with your community by organizing a canned goods drive for a local food bank or serving on the board of your local crisis pregnancy center; you can share your resources with those in need by giving clothes and furniture to homeless shelters and donating money to disaster relief projects sponsored by LCMS World Relief and Human Care. Whatever it is you have to give, the opportunities for serving your neighbor are truly endless. All you need to do is look around and ask "Where am I?" and "Who is my neighbor?" and "What does she need?" You'll know exactly what to do.

My Hope Is Built on Nothing Less
> My hope is built on nothing less
> Than Jesus' blood and righteousness;
> No merit of my own I claim
> But wholly lean on Jesus' name.
> On Christ, the solid rock, I stand;
> All other ground is sinking sand.
>
> His oath, His covenant and blood
> Support me in the raging flood;
> When ev'ry earthly prop gives way,
> He then is all my hope and stay.
> On Christ, the solid rock, I stand;
> All other ground is sinking sand. (*LSB* 575:1, 3)

Collect

Lord, through Your Word, You created the world. Through that same Word, Jesus Christ, You saved all of creation on the cross. Help us to trust in the power of that Word still today, knowing that You who feeds the lowly sparrows, clothes the grass with lilies, and upholds the entire universe, will continue to preserve, sustain, and support us unto life everlasting, whatever storms may come; through Jesus Christ, the Word of God incarnate. Amen.

Session Four

FAYE

Make a joyful noise to the LORD, all the earth!
>   Serve the LORD with gladness!
>   Come into His presence with singing!
Know that the LORD, He is God!
>   It is He who made us, and we are His;
>   we are His people, and the sheep of His pasture.
Enter His gates with thanksgiving,
>   and His courts with praise!
>   Give thanks to Him; bless His name!
For the LORD is good;
>   His steadfast love endures forever,
>   and His faithfulness to all generations. Psalm 100

"Watercolor is loose," Faye often told her students. "It can escape from you."

Faye knew a bit about taming fluid colors. For over seventy years she wielded a paintbrush, training fickle blues, reds, yellows, and greens into pastoral scenes. She liked the intrinsic contrasts in watercolor, the darkening of shadows to bring out the light and the softening of lines to better define the significance of a composition.

Landscapes were her favorite. Faye could lose herself in the story of a painting. She liked to imagine the sound of the birds singing in the rendered oak trees, the feel of the sun shining on a wash of golden-green pasture, and the smell of wildflowers growing near an old barn painted on a hill. There was no greater pleasure in life for Faye than re-creating God's natural earth on a sheet of clothlike paper.

That is why the change in her eyesight was so distressing.

Faye first noticed something was wrong one day while she was driving. Roads that had always been straight began to curve and weave along her field of vision. Color betrayed her next. Yellows started looking like pinks, and blues and greens became almost indistinguishable. Faye felt particularly defeated one morning to discover that the burnt sienna she had just brushed onto her paper looked more like red lipstick than rust. She fearfully set her brush back down onto the table.

"You need to see a retina specialist—right now," Faye's eye doctor informed her.

The retina specialist's diagnosis was swift. "It is macular degeneration. Blood vessels are leaking fluid into the inside of your eye, and, as the retina changes, your color discrimination also changes." The specialist gave Faye a shot directly in her left eye in an attempt to reduce the leakage of the vessels. Unfortunately, the shot resulted in an infection, and Faye's left eye retained debris that further clouded her vision. The specialist held little hope that Faye would regain the sight she had lost, and he even warned that her vision would most likely get worse.

Faye sat in her living room, demoralized at the prospect of a colorless future. What would she do? How would she fill her time? For the better part of her life, watercolor painting had been her natural talent, her cultured skill, and her self-expression all rolled into one. Without it, her life was simply unrecognizable.

Faye turned to look at a painting hanging over her living room fireplace. It was a winter scene of a wooded ravine. The naked bark of the trees reflected the crystalline glow of the snowy sunshine, and a frosty lake steamed far off in the distance. She had painted that scene years ago, and it still pleased her today to see how far back in the tree line she had achieved definition. What a thrill it was to design a composition, to outline where the darks and lights should go, and then to fill in pools of color and have it come out exactly right. Would she ever be able to paint like that again?

Loyce, Faye's lifelong friend and roommate, stood in the doorway to the kitchen, silently watching as the past and future made a battleground of Faye's present. She walked into the living room to try to ease her friend's burden. "The afternoon light is good in the studio. Do you think you'll paint today?"

Faye shook her head. "I've lost the truth in my vision, and now I have no desire to paint."

"Maybe just sitting in the studio will make you feel like it."

"Loyce," Faye started, covering her right eye with her hand, "do you know what I see out of this eye? I see objects with no definition, no depth, and no interest. I see nothing worth painting."

"Then, let's go find something worth painting. How about we drive through the country?"

"It's just not the same," Faye said. "It's almost as if I have lost an eye. There's no longer any depth perception, no dimension to the world. Everything has flattened out. Where's the inspiration in a flat world?"

Loyce grieved for her friend. The two women had roomed together since their college days, and Loyce had watched

Faye grow from a young art student to an accomplished artist. She had been present for Faye's first exhibit, her first commission, and her first Best in Show. Neither woman ever expected to face a day when Faye could no longer paint.

As the months passed, Loyce noticed that Faye's eyesight was not the only thing to diminish. Portions of Faye's memory began to fade into darkness, leaving pockets of life missing like chapters torn from a book. Routine became the careful guide which directed the course of her days. Faye rarely painted anymore, yet she seemed less angry these days to be parted from her beloved art. The memory loss had taken the edge off of most things in her life, but it was more than that. Faye possessed a comfort and assurance that went beyond watercolors and paintbrushes.

"You know," Faye offered one morning, her eyes shining particularly bright, "painting is important, but it is not the most important. It can't be. It doesn't last."

"What is most important then?" Loyce knew the answer, but she still wanted to hear it.

"The things that last," Faye said. "God; His Church; the love He shows to me in Jesus; the faithful friend He has given me in you. Those are the most important, and I don't have to paint them or even see them to know that.

"Here's the way I see it," Faye winked, the memory loss clearly not affecting her sense of humor. "I miss painting, but I also miss driving and playing bridge and a bunch of other things that fade away." Faye looked over at her winter scene hanging above the fireplace. She could barely make out the definition she had always admired in the extending tree line, but no matter. "My paintings and my eyesight may even fade away, but the love of the Lord endures forever. That is most important."

STUDY QUESTIONS

1. What do you fear losing the most?

2. What comfort do we have in the face of loss?

3. The psalmist sings of God's faithfulness (Psalm 100:5). How has God been faithful to all generations?

4. Faye realized that her paintings would not last forever. Which things do last forever? How do we know this? (Hebrews 13:8)

5. What is most important in Faye's life and the life of every Christian? Is this "most important" thing something we can ever lose?

6. How does the First Commandment, "You shall have no other gods," help refocus our lives on what is most important?

7. Loyce is a faithful friend to Faye. How can we be faithful friends to our brothers and sisters in Christ who suffer from loss?

8. Turn to the hymns 741–765, the "Hope and Comfort" section of *Lutheran Service Book*. Which hymns do you find comforting? Pick one hymn text to memorize this week.

_____

_____

_____

_____

_____

_____

A MOMENT IN THE PEW

Loss comes in all shapes and sizes. Some women lose their homes, others lose their families, and others still, like Faye, lose their health and hobbies. Although our losses maybe different, our comfort remains the same: we have been made alive forever in Christ Jesus, and nothing—not even the loss of what we hold most dear—can separate us from God's love.

We, as pew sisters, are the perfect ambassadors of comfort to each other in our seasons of loss because we all know and understand the constancy and consolation of Christ's forgiveness and love. We have the Words of eternal life, namely Scripture, to speak to each other in times of grief and sorrow, and we know exactly where to direct each other to find Christ's strengthening gifts: church, to hear His Word and to receive His body and blood. We also know how to listen to each other with patience and kindness, being careful not to tell each other how to feel but, instead, encouraging each other every day through acts of mercy. Like Loyce, we can be faithful friends in times of loss, ready with a listening ear, a steadying hand, and a caring heart.

HYMN STANZAS FOR MEDITATION

Abide with Me
    Swift to its close ebbs out life's little day;
    Earth's joys grow dim, its glories pass away;
    Change and decay in all around I see;
    O Thou who changest not, abide with me.

    Hold Thou Thy cross before my closing eyes;
    Shine through the gloom,
        and point me to the skies.
    Heav'n's morning breaks,
        and earth's vain shadows flee;
    In life, in death, O Lord, abide with me.
    (*LSB* 878:4, 6)

Collect

Lord God, You are faithful to all generations through
the sacrifice of Your own Son, Jesus. Assure us with
Your Holy Spirit that we are most important to You,
now and forevermore, and comfort us with Your
everlasting love that we might enter Your gates with
thanksgiving, even as the things of this life fade away;
through Jesus Christ, our Lord. Amen.

EMILY

For Moses writes about the righteousness that is based on the law, that the person who does the commandments shall live by them. But the righteousness based on faith says, "Do not say in your heart, 'Who will ascend into heaven?'" (that is, to bring Christ down) or "'Who will descend into the abyss?'" (that is, to bring Christ up from the dead). But what does it say? "The word is near you, in your mouth and in your heart" (that is, the word of faith that we proclaim); because, if you confess with your mouth that Jesus is Lord and believe in your heart that God raised Him from the dead, you will be saved. Romans 10:5–9

Emily feared that she was not good enough.

It started back in middle school when her pastor invited all of the sinners in church to come to the altar to be saved. Emily knew she would never get to heaven by staying seated in the pews, so she carried her transgressing heart down the aisle to get some salvation.

Still, something was not quite right. No matter how hard Emily tried to do all of the things her pastor preached from the pulpit, she never seemed to be able to keep a perfect score. Love her neighbor? It was impossible to love the boy in PE who yelled at her for dropping the ball. Honor her father and mother? No one should have to make her bed every morning. Don't covet your neighbor? It was unfair that her sister got the last scoop of ice cream. Emily knew she was coming up short on God's to-do list, and she began to doubt whether she was even saved. Afraid for her eternal life, she marched down to the altar time and time again to get some more of that salvation, just to be sure.

But Emily wasn't sure. Even as an adult, she feared that she was still not good enough.

"What's the matter?" her husband Matthew asked one Sunday morning as they walked out of church.

Emily sighed. "I just don't feel like I belong in there."

"Why?"

"Oh, I don't know," Emily shrugged. "Everyone in there just seems so perfect. They have the perfect smile, the perfect hair, the perfect life. They don't seem to make any mistakes. It makes me feel like I have to have it altogether all of the time, or I'm not a good Christian."

Matthew nodded. "I know what you mean. One of the band members backstage asked me how I was doing before the service. I started to tell him that I was kind of stressed out at work, and he got really uncomfortable. He told me that I needed to pray more about my job."

Emily frowned. "It's like you can't even have a bad day, or you don't really have Christ in your life. That just doesn't seem right to me. Either we're really messed up, or they've all got it wrong."

"Or both," Matthew cracked a smile.

"Whatever it is, I'm tired of walking out of church more stressed and drained than when I walked in."

The next Sunday, Matthew and Emily tried a different church across town.

"This is small," Emily whispered, looking around at the people greeting one another in the pews. She was used to worshiping in an auditorium filled with thousands of strangers. Here, there were no more than two hundred people in attendance, and they all seemed to know one another.

The size of the congregation wasn't the only thing that was different in this church.

"Christianity is not about having the perfect life," Pastor Murphy preached from the pulpit. "Jesus and His disciples suffered when they walked this earth, and you can expect to suffer too. You are going to have bad days. You might get angry in traffic on your morning commute, feel jealous of your co-worker's new vacation home, or simply wake up on the wrong side of the bed. You might lose your job, your house, your family, even your happiness, but none of those losses is a reflection of your relationship with God. You and He are good. You can trust that God loves you and is merciful to you because He tells us so in His Word: 'For God so loved the world, that He gave His only Son, that whoever believes in Him should not perish but have eternal life' (John 3:16). Believe, people of God, and know that whether you have a good day or a bad day, you are still good with God because of what Jesus did for you on the cross."

Emily and Matthew walked out of church that morning stunned by joy. They sat speechless in the car for a few moments before Matthew finally cleared his throat and started the car. "Um, I think we should come back. What do you think?"

Emily smiled, lighthearted for the first time in months; no, in years. She still felt unsure of whether or not she was good enough to meet God's standards, but she knew that Pastor Murphy had told her the truth from God's Word that morning. She couldn't wait to come back for more.

The next week, Emily and Matthew not only attended the church across town again, but they also joined the adult instruction class taught by Pastor Murphy. They couldn't get enough of his teaching about God's grace, mercy, and love in Christ Jesus. They feasted on his lessons like starved children at a royal banquet.

"It is all about subject-verb agreement," Pastor Murphy explained in class. "Listen to your pastor and make sure he is putting the pronouns in all of the right places. God always does the action for us, not the other way around. He is the subject, and we are the direct and indirect objects. God creates us, loves us, saves us, redeems us, forgives us, preserves us, and sustains us. God gives us Jesus and makes us His children. God is always the subject when it comes to our salvation and life in Him, and we are simply the objects which receive His gracious actions."

That night, Matthew and Emily recited their nightly prayers together.

"God, I just want to tell You how much I love You—" Emily spoke aloud, but she stopped at the gentle touch of her husband's hand on her arm.

"I'm sorry, honey," Matthew apologized. "I don't mean to stop you, but I think this is a good moment for us to work on our subject-verb agreement like Pastor Murphy said."

"What do you mean?"

"Well, I mean that it is not so important that you love God—"

"But I do!"

"Yes, I know you do," Matthew said carefully, "but you can love God only because He loved you first. Everything we say teaches us what to believe, so I think it is better to practice reminding ourselves that God is the One who loves us."

Emily practiced putting God in the subject of her sentences, and, as a result, began focusing on all that He did and was still doing for her. What great comfort and joy she experienced as the direct object of Christ's loving action! No doubt, she still fell short on God's to-do list, but He never fell short when it came to providing for her. She found herself listening closely to everyone speaking around her to find out where they were putting God in their sentences.

"Emily," a friend from her former church texted her one day, "would you please pray that I might cling to the Lord during this difficult time?"

Emily picked up her phone, eager to respond. For the first time, she knew exactly what to write to bring true comfort to her friend. "God is already clinging to you. You don't have to worry about holding onto Him. He is right there with you, and He won't let go."

"What do you mean by that?" was her friend's instant reply. "Do you think I don't have enough faith to hold onto Him?"

Emily blanched. She hadn't meant to insult her friend. She was just trying to relieve her of her burden, to assure her of God's faithfulness to her at all times. "No," she quickly replied, "I just meant that God is faithful to you always in Christ."

"I already know that. I've always known that."

Emily didn't know why this was going wrong. She held her phone, uncertain of what to say.

"I think your new church is warping you," came the next message. "Don't forget what it means to be a Christian. I pray that you will be able to hold onto your faith in God through all of this. Don't let them turn you into a judgmental monster."

Matthew walked into the room at that moment and found his wife crying on the couch. "What happened?"

Emily tried to explain.

"I think you should call Pastor Murphy."

"He'd take the time to talk with me about this?" Emily had never heard of such a thing. Her whole life, she had attended churches where the pastors were too busy and important to be available to the individual congregants.

"That's what he's there for," Matthew encouraged.

Pastor Murphy not only talked with Emily on the phone, but he suggested that Emily come to his office to talk through her problem with her friend.

"Isn't it interesting," Pastor Murphy leaned his elbows on his desk, "how people react negatively when we challenge their fleshly desire to make their faith about themselves?"

Emily thought about what he said. "It comes down to subject-verb agreement, doesn't it?"

Pastor Murphy smiled and nodded.

"You know," Emily confided, "for so many years I have made my faith about what I do for God. I always put myself as the subject doing the action. I thought that being a Christian meant doing more of this and less of that to be close to God, that it was all up to me to keep proving to

God and to everyone else that I was a believer. I thought that doing good works was a way to wave my hand at God to get His attention."

"God is not so concerned with looking at your good works," Pastor Murphy said. "Instead, He wants to show you Christ's good work on the cross for your salvation."

Emily nodded her head, understanding.

"The Bible tells us that our own 'righteous deeds are like a polluted garment' (Isaiah 64:6). Our own good works are filthy by nature and can never make us righteous before God. It is only Christ's perfect work on the cross that makes us righteous," Pastor Murphy said. He opened his Bible. "Paul writes in his epistle to the Romans, 'for all have sinned and fall short of the glory of God, and are justified freely by His grace as a gift, through the redemption that is in Christ Jesus, whom God put forward as a propitiation by His blood, to be received by faith' (Romans 3:23–25). Do you see what Paul is saying? Christ's redemption is what makes you righteous, and it is God's gift to you. He is the One waving His hand to get your attention, so that He can give you this gift to save you from your sins."

"How do I get this gift?" Emily asked, thinking back to all of the altar calls of her youth.

"Are you baptized?"

"Yes, more times than I'd like to count."

"Well, it's that first Baptism in the name of the Father and of the Son and of the Holy Spirit that did it. That's when God gave you Christ's righteousness." Pastor Murphy's eyes gleamed with the privilege of sharing the Gospel with this young woman. "Emily, hear God's promise to you in the Book of Galatians: 'For as many of you as were baptized into Christ have put on Christ. . . . And if you are

Christ's, then you are Abraham's offspring, heirs according to the promise'" (Galatians 3:27, 29).

An heir!

"You put on Christ in your Baptism, Emily, and you were made an heir of God's promises. You were written into His will, so to speak, and now everything that is Christ's is yours, even eternal life."

Emily sighed with relief as she realized the truth. She didn't have to be good enough to get to heaven. Christ was good enough for both of them.

STUDY QUESTIONS

1. What is righteousness?

2. Moses writes about the righteousness that is based on the Law. Can we become righteous through keeping the Law?

3. How do we become righteous?

4. What is this righteousness based on faith of which Paul writes in his epistle to the Romans?

----

5. We Lutherans like to talk about Law and Gospel. What is the Law? What is the Gospel? How can we properly distinguish between the two when reading God's Word and hearing it proclaimed?

----

6. Why is it important to always put God in the subject whenever we talk about salvation and our life in the Church?

----

7. Why is it so tempting to put ourselves in the subject
   and focus on what we do for God and His kingdom?
   Why is it a privilege to be the direct object of God's
   action?

   _____

   _____

   _____

   _____

   _____

8. Focusing on our own good works leads to despair.
   On what, instead, should we focus?

   _____

   _____

   _____

   _____

   _____

A MOMENT IN THE PEW

We hear a lot about "Law" and "Gospel" from our pastors in the pulpit, but what in the world do these two words actually mean and how do they apply to Scripture? Simply put, everything in the Word of God that tells us *to do* something is Law, and everything in God's Word that tells us what Christ *has done* for us is Gospel. Think of it this way: the Law is a command, the Gospel is a pardon; the Law condemns, the Gospel saves; the Law shows us our sin, the Gospel shows us Jesus. Can you see why it is so important to get the distinction between the two correct? The difference is our salvation.

We can be tempted to read Scripture as a handbook for how to live the life of a Christian, focusing primarily on the Law, which tells us what to do and what not to do. However, strictly reading the Bible as Law is both incorrect and dangerous, for it ignores Jesus and all that He has done for us to redeem us, to reconcile us to the Father, and to strengthen us with His Spirit. It thumbs our noses at Jesus on the cross.

Martin Luther warns that living life by the Law will lead to one of two terrible things: despair, because we cannot properly do all that God commands, or pride, because we become puffed up by tallying our own "good" works. Yet, we know from the Book of Isaiah that our own works are anything but good (see Isaiah 64:6). They are as dirty as the rags we toss in the trash. Thankfully, God does not leave us to despair in our own filth brought on by the Law—He also gives us the sweet Gospel in His Word: Christ's good works are righteous, and His righteousness was applied to our filth in our Baptism; we are washed clean forever in Jesus. May God help all of us in the pews to live by the Gospel, not by the Law!

Not What These Hands Have Done
Not what these hands have done
Can save this guilty soul;
Not what this toiling flesh has borne
Can make my spirit whole.

Not what I feel or do
Can give me peace with God;
Not all my prayers and sighs and tears
Can bear my awful load.

Thy work alone, O Christ,
Can ease this weight of sin;
Thy blood alone, O Lamb of God,
Can give me peace within.

Thy love to me, O God,
Not mine, O Lord, to Thee,
Can rid me of this dark unrest
And set my spirit free. (*LSB* 567:1–4)

Collect

Lord God, we will never be good enough on our own. Our goodness is as filthy rags, our good works are meaningless, and our toiling under the sun is a chasing after the wind. Wash clean our filth, good Savior, in the waters of Holy Baptism. Give meaning to our works, O Lord, with the gift of faith in You. Redeem our toiling, Holy One, through Your sacrifice on the cross, and make Your goodness our own; through Jesus Christ, Your Son, our Lord, who lives and reigns with You and Holy Spirit, one God, now and forever. Amen.

Session Six

ANNA

I lift up my eyes to the hills.
>From where does my help come?
My help comes from the LORD,
>who made heaven and earth.
He will not let your foot be moved;
>He who keeps you will not slumber.
Behold, He who keeps Israel
>will neither slumber nor sleep.
The LORD is your keeper;
>the LORD is your shade on your right hand.
The sun shall not strike you by day,
>nor the moon by night.
The LORD will keep you from all evil;
>He will keep your life.
The LORD will keep
>your going out and your coming in
>from this time forth and forevermore. Psalm 121

Anna sat on her hospital bed, the incision from her cesarean not even a day old. Nurses had whisked baby Elizabeth away to the neonatal intensive care unit promptly after her delivery. Elizabeth was having a little trouble breathing, but Anna was not worried. It was common for C-section babies to have breathing issues, and she knew her baby was in the hands of caring, competent professionals.

"What is it?" Anna asked the NICU doctor upon seeing his sober expression.

"Elizabeth has a heart murmur."

Anna's face grew white.

"Now, don't worry," the doctor quickly reassured her. "It is most likely just a hole in her heart. Lots of babies have them, and the holes usually close up on their own."

Elizabeth's pediatrician ordered an echocardiogram just to be sure. Anna knew things were bad when a cardiologist walked through her hospital room door. She began to cry before he even spoke a word.

"Elizabeth has a valve problem . . ." the cardiologist began, but Anna barely heard anything else he said. She remembered him drawing visual aids on a picture of a heart, but she couldn't make out the images through all of her tears. She caught something about a big right ventricle and blood bypassing her baby's lungs, but all she could think over and over again in her head was, "This is a dream. This can't be happening."

"Will she live?" Anna asked, her voice thick.

"Elizabeth requires heart surgery to live," the cardiologist answered.

Anna felt the air closing in around her. "What will be her quality of life after the surgery?"

"There are people living with tetralogy today who are in their twenties."

"Not older?"

"This surgery has only been in existence for that long," the cardiologist admitted.

Anna was painfully aware of all that the cardiologist was not promising. The truth of his silence struck a terror deep in her heart. "Oh, God!" she silently cried, her fears too monstrous to tame into actual petitions.

Anna cried uncontrollably for hours. That night, a kind nurse walked her up and down the halls of the hospital, but, still, she couldn't rest. Sleep and all of it comforts had been stripped from her, and Anna knew they would never fully return until her little girl was okay.

"Elizabeth needs to be at twelve pounds before we can operate," the cardiologist informed Anna and her husband the next day. "If she can gain another five pounds in the next six months, we may be able to operate before Christmas."

Anna nodded her head, resolute. Her tears had hardened to tenacity overnight, and this mama bear was raring to go. Five pounds was all that stood in the way of her little cub's health and vitality. She would do this. She had to.

Several weeks later, Elizabeth's pediatrician asked, "What's the matter?"

Anna tried hard to hold back her frustration. "Something's wrong. Elizabeth will only take a bottle if she is sleeping. If she wakes up, she won't eat at all. When she does stay asleep, it still takes us two hours to get only two ounces of formula in her before she wakes up again." Anna ran her hand through her hair in exasperation. The number *12* was emblazoned onto the backs of her eyelids, and all she could see was her own failure if her baby girl didn't gain enough weight in time.

"How often are you feeding her?" the pediatrician asked.

"We feed her for two hours straight, and then we only have one hour off before we have to start the process all over again."

"And that means none of you are sleeping."

Anna nodded her head, biting her lip. "Jeff takes the night shift, and then I take over at four in the morning so he can sleep a bit before work. We feed her all day and night because we have no other option. It's a mess."

The pediatrician sat and watched while Anna gave Elizabeth a bottle in the office. "I've never seen anything like it," he whispered as Elizabeth, asleep, slowly suckled the bottle. "I'm not sure why she is eating this way. Maybe it is her heart, but, whatever the reason, she needs to gain weight. If this is the only way she will eat, then so be it. Do you think you can keep this going for five more months?"

Mama Bear gritted her teeth and nodded her head.

Anna's parents started bringing dinner over every night, and, on some occasions, Anna's father stayed the night to feed Elizabeth so Anna and Jeff could catch some sleep. Elizabeth slowly grew, but she also slowly grew used to being held. Any time her parents tried to set her down, she started to fuss and cry. Anna pined for the day when she could train her child without the risk of her daughter turning blue. In the meantime, she faithfully held Elizabeth to keep her oxygen levels high.

The day before the surgery, Elizabeth was admitted into the hospital for a heart catheterization.

"Thirteen pounds!" the doctor exclaimed, impressed.

Anna was almost too tired to celebrate.

"And that's not all," the doctor said. "We found a vascular ring restricting Elizabeth's esophagus during the catheterization."

"Is that why she only eats when she's asleep?"

"It wouldn't surprise me. We can easily cut the ring out during Elizabeth's surgery tomorrow, and that should release the pressure on her esophagus."

Anna was not too tired to celebrate that!

The next morning, Anna and Jeff kissed Elizabeth one more time before letting the nurses wheel her away for open-heart surgery. For the next seven hours, their heads and hearts were too filled with their baby girl to think or feel much of anything else. When the surgeon finally came to the waiting room at the end of the ordeal, they jumped up from their seats.

"Everything went well," he said, smiling easily. "I was able to patch the hole in her heart and open up the pulmonary valve. I was even able to cut out that curious, vascular ring."

The nurses wheeled Elizabeth's tiny, anesthetized body to the pediatric cardiovascular ICU, and Anna and Jeff stood guard on either side, touching their miracle baby's tiny hands. It had been such a long road, but here they were at the turn in the bend. For months, all Anna had been able to see was the roadblock ahead, but, now that the surgery was over, she dreamed about the untraveled road stretching promisingly before her daughter. Elizabeth would live, and the enormity of God's goodness to her tiny daughter threatened to overwhelm Anna's senses. "Oh, God!" she silently cried again, this time her joy too rich and full for words.

"She did just fine," the ICU nurse chirped, her lips curling with a Swedish accent.

Anna nodded.

"Now, we just let her rest. I bet you two could use some rest yourselves."

Anna and Jeff still held their baby's hands.

"I am glad she was born," Anna whispered. She felt pure gratitude to be Elizabeth's mother, and, as she turned to look at her husband, an even deeper truth resounded in her heart. "No, I am so glad she was born to us."

Jeff smiled. For hours, days, weeks, and months, he and Anna had toiled together to keep their daughter alive. They were the perfect team, really, and it was all worth it in the end. "We take really good care of her, don't we?"

"How about I take really good care of her for both of you tonight?" the nurse offered. She looked Anna in the eye, and Anna knew she could trust this woman. Elizabeth would be safe under her watch. "I've got everything under control here. You two go on home and get some sleep."

Anna didn't need to be told twice.

STUDY QUESTIONS

1. Just like Elizabeth, we are each born with a "hole" in our heart that does not heal on its own. What causes this hole? What heals it?

2. Anna and Jeff faithfully cared for their sick daughter, even when her needs caused them pain and grief. How is this a picture of how our own heavenly Father faithfully cares for us?

3. Reflecting on Luther's meaning of the First Article of the Apostles' Creed, in what ways does God provide for you?

_____

_____

_____

_____

_____

_____

I believe that God has made me and all creatures; that He has given me my body and soul, eyes, ears, and all my members, my reason and all my senses, and still takes care of them.

He also gives me clothing and shoes, food and drink, house and home, wife and children, land, animals, and all I have. He richly and daily provides me with all that I need to support this body and life.

He defends me against all danger and guards and protects me from all evil.

All this He does only out of fatherly, divine goodness and mercy, without any merit or worthiness in me. For all this it is my duty to thank and praise, serve and obey Him.

This is most certainly true.

(Small Catechism, First Article)

4. Elizabeth's parents fed her day and night to keep her alive. God sustains and preserves our lives in Him day and night. How does He do this?

5. What are we asking from God when we petition in the Lord's Prayer, "give us this day our daily bread"?

6. God used Anna's parents to help care for Anna, Jeff, and Elizabeth's physical needs. How does God use the Church to help provide for the physical needs of others?

7. Anna and Jeff stayed up night and day to make sure their daughter was properly fed. God neither slumbers nor sleeps but, instead, promises to keep you all your life. How can this comfort us in our times of fear and doubt?

8. In Luther's morning and evening prayers (page 82), we acknowledge that God is indeed the One who keeps us day and night. We also petition God in these prayers to "let [His] holy angel be with me, that the evil foe may have no power over me." What a comforting petition to pray in the face of our fears and doubts! Memorize these prayers and use them daily.

A MOMENT IN THE PEW

D o you ever feel like you can't relate to what a pew sister's going through? Do you feel intimidated by the enormity of her particular trial? Do you balk at the thought of approaching her in her pain and grief? Are you afraid you won't know what to say?

Well, you don't have to say anything. Just be there. Take care of her needs. Make sure her pastor knows what is going on so that he can go to her and minister to her. Pray for her and her family. Bring her chocolates and flowers and lasagna. Fluff her pillows and make her some tea. Take her out for a pedicure. Send her a card that will make her laugh. Buy her some comfy slippers and take her dog for a walk. Watch her children while she steals a quick nap. Take her crying baby out of church so that she can remain seated and listen to the Word that is being preached for her benefit. Make sure she has no reason to miss the adult Sunday School class or the midweek Bible class. Visit her on the anniversary of her particular loss. Sit with her while she waits for whatever is coming. Smile at her and thank her for her friendship. Ask her some questions and listen to her answers. Whatever you do, don't be afraid. Sharing in her sorrows is the same as sharing in her joys. All you need to do is be there for the sharing.

HYMN STANZA FOR MEDITATION

If Thou But Trust in God to Guide Thee
>If thou but trust in God to guide thee
>And hope in Him through all thy ways,
>He'll give thee strength, whate'er betide thee,
>And bear thee through the evil days.
>Who trusts in God's unchanging love
>Builds on the rock that naught can move.
>(*LSB* 750:1)

Collect

I thank You, my heavenly Father, through Jesus Christ, Your dear Son, that You have kept me this night from all harm and danger; and I pray that You would keep me this day also from sin and every evil, that all my doings and life may please You. For into Your hands I commend myself, my body and soul, and all things. Let Your holy angel be with me, that the evil foe may have no power over me. Amen. (Small Catechism, Morning Prayer)

I thank You, my heavenly Father, through Jesus Christ, Your dear Son, that You have graciously kept me this day; and I pray that You would forgive me all my sins where I have done wrong, and graciously keep me this night. For into Your hands I commend myself, my body and soul, and all things. Let Your holy angel be with me, that the evil foe may have no power over me. Amen. (Small Catechism, Evening Prayer)

Session Seven

DIEDRE

Love is patient and kind; love does not envy or boast;
it is not arrogant or rude. It does not insist on its own
way; it is not irritable or resentful; it does not rejoice at
wrongdoing, but rejoices with the truth. Love bears all
things, believes all things, hopes all things, endures all
things. Love never ends. 1 Corinthians 13:4–8

Women never retire. There is always someone who needs
their care.

Diedre knew this all too well. The moment she pulled into
the church parking lot, her cell phone rang. It was her
husband.

"This is Hans."

"Yes, Hans, I know it's you."

"Where are you?"

"I'm at church. Tonight is the Lydia Circle meeting."

"Why didn't you tell me you had a meeting?"

"I did. I told you this afternoon. Look by the phone.
I wrote it down on a note for you. This is my month to
provide the dessert."

Silence. "There's something wrong here."

"What?"

"I don't know. The dog was barking."

"Well, he might have seen a squirrel or something like that."

"I think someone was trying to get in the house."

Diedre sat still, disappointed and frustrated. She had only been gone from home ten minutes, and already Hans was calling her. He always called. He scared so easily these days, but it wasn't really his fault. The stroke had attacked his upper right temporal lobe, the part of the brain that handles memory, emotion, and motivation.

"I'll be home in a minute." Diedre ended the call and sighed. She had been looking forward to this meeting all day. She had even made pie. She was almost certain no one was trying to break into their house, but she didn't want Hans to feel abandoned. If she went home, he would calm down. He always felt secure when she was around. Diedre walked the golden-crusted pies into the church and then turned around to drive back home to her husband.

Later that week, Hans woke Diedre in the middle of the night.

"I need to go to the bathroom."

Diedre helped Hans out of bed and into the bathroom. It was 1:15. "Hey, today is June 4. Fifty years ago today, we were getting married." She leaned down to clean her husband's behind. "Do you think this is the 'for better' or the 'for worse' part?"

Hans didn't miss a beat. "I guess it depends on your outlook."

Diedre leaned against the bathroom wall and laughed, hard. Every once in awhile, her husband's quick wit and sense of humor beamed through the confusion, and she caught a glimpse of the man with whom she had fallen madly in love.

Still, the road was rough and both of them were weary.

"Do you think I am going to end up like Ingrid?" Hans whispered in the dark after he was safely back in bed.

Diedre's heart broke at the sound of fear in her husband's voice. Ingrid, Hans' sister, had been suffering from Alzheimer's for the past seven years.

"No, Hans," Diedre managed lightly, hiding the emotion in her voice, "it's only the women in your family who get Alzheimer's, and that's because they have to live with the men."

This time Hans was the one who laughed.

The next day bloomed bright and sunny. Robins perched in the crape myrtle trees outside their living room window, but the sights and sounds of spring did nothing to ease the heaviness in Diedre's heart. Her husband was slowly slipping away from her, and the reality of what was ahead cut through her soul like a dagger. Hans had always been the most tender-hearted husband, loving father, and brilliant physics teacher, but it was getting harder to see his virtues through all of the bathroom episodes and medication battles.

"I'm taking a walk, Hans," Diedre called on her way out the door. She walked agitatedly down the sidewalk, blind to the beauty of the morning. She looked up toward the bright, blue sky and prayed, "Please, God! There has to be something better than this for Hans. His whole world is just getting smaller and smaller. Something needs to change!"

Two weeks later, Diedre found herself lying on a hospital bed.

"Well," the doctor said, "the catheterization shows your arteries to be clear as a bell, but there is also evidence of heart failure."

"I don't understand."

The doctor looked up from his chart. "You had a heart attack."

"I *did?*" Diedre was flabbergasted. She sure couldn't remember ever having a heart attack. Wouldn't she have noticed such a thing? "When? Why?"

"I'm not exactly sure. Honestly, I think you might be suffering from broken-heart syndrome."

Diedre looked at her doctor skeptically. He seemed qualified. At least, he was wearing one of those white coats.

The doctor explained, "People who have been caretakers for long periods of time sometimes have temporary heart complications related to stress. Tell me, Mrs. Flanders, how long have you been looking after your husband?"

Diedre was hesitant. "It's been thirteen years since his stroke."

The doctor nodded his head. "I think we are going to have to find a way for you to get more rest. You can't take care of your husband all by yourself. You need some help."

Diedre was resistant, but her son, Don, took matters into his own hands. He moved his parents into an assisted living facility where Hans could receive twenty-four-hour care and Diedre could sleep in her own apartment each night.

"I know it's hard, Mom," Don sympathized, "but it's time. You can still spend all day with Dad, but you also need some time to rest and recharge. For years, you have been caring for everyone else around you and neglecting yourself. Not anymore."

Diedre wasn't convinced. Hans needed her. He got upset if she was gone for too long, and he never seemed interested in doing anything with anybody else. His world was already so restricted. He would never understand why she was gone at night.

Don helped Diedre out of the car and into her new apartment.

"Where's your dad?" Diedre asked, looking around.

"He's just fine. He's being taken care of."

"I want to see him."

Don nodded. He walked his mother to an open room on the first floor of the facility. Diedre stopped short in the doorway, her right hand flying up to cover her mouth. She could not believe what she was seeing. There sat Hans in his wheelchair in a big circle with the other residents, bouncing a balloon back and forth with his new friends. He had the biggest smile on his face.

Diedre's eyes filled with tears. She had been afraid this new arrangement would not work, but Hans looked so happy. Perhaps Don was right. Maybe this was all for the best, not just for her but also for her dear husband.

God had answered her prayers, just not in the way she expected.

STUDY QUESTIONS

1. What is love? What is love *not*?

_____

_____

_____

_____

2. Verse 13 of 1 Corinthians 13 reads, "So now faith, hope, and love abide, these three; but the greatest of these is love." Faith and hope, given to us by God, help ourselves. Whom does love help?

_____

_____

_____

_____

3. Diedre cared for her husband by herself for thirteen years. In a long-term-care situation, bearing all things and enduring all things can be the most difficult part of love. What are ways our faith can be fed and strengthened during these marathon times?

_____

_____

_____

4. God commands all of us in His Word to serve our neighbor. Who is our neighbor?

5. Vocation is a word the Church uses to describe the various roles in which God has placed us to properly serve our neighbors. Some of us are daughters, sisters, wives, mothers, friends, teachers, librarians, grocery clerks, you name it. What are some of your vocations? What special ways has God given you to serve your neighbor in these vocations?

6. There are times when our neighbor's need surpasses the care we can give her. How can we know when it is time to let go and seek help in giving care?

7. Sometimes, we are the ones in need of care. How can we be supportive and loving to the caretaker God gives to us?

8. Why does love never end?

A MOMENT IN THE PEW

Your vocations are the specific roles in which God has placed you at this particular point in time to love and care for your brothers and sisters in Christ. Do you ever wish you had a different vocation? Do you envy the mother with the newborn baby or the business woman with the high-rise office? It can be hard not to compare your own life's vocations with those of your sisters in Christ, but we are not called to compare the work of one member of the Body with another. "Now there are varieties of gifts, but the same Spirit; and there are varieties of service, but the same Lord; and there are varieties of activities, but it is the same God who empowers them all in everyone. To each is given the manifestation of the Spirit for the common good" (1 Corinthians 12:4–7).

You have been called to love God and serve your neighbor right where you are. If everyone worked in a skyscraper, then there would be no one to teach the Kindergarten Sunday School class or to change the baby's diaper or to coach the swim team. Remember, "God arranged the members in the body, each one of them, as He chose. If all were a single member, where would the body be?" (1 Corinthians 12:18–19) You are an important part of the Body of Christ, designed specifically by God to serve your neighbor in a specific way, and you are needed just as you are, whether you are an eye, an ear, a hand, or a little toe.

Caregiving is one example of a God-given vocation, and caregivers, especially those like Diedre who are in it for the long haul, are in need of our love and support. Surely we can faithfully pray for them, that God would strengthen and preserve their faith in Him through all trial and tribulation, but we also can give these servants of mercy our time and attention to help ease the burden they carry. We can visit them, bringing a friendly smile and a listening ear to their front door. We can send them a card, cook them a meal, and buy them a new jigsaw puzzle. We can offer them precious hours of respite, standing in to care for their loved one while they go grocery shopping or take in a movie. We can invite them out for coffee or lunch and include them in our church social activities. We can greet them every Sunday in church and inquire about their needs. Whatever it is we do to love and serve them in our privileged vocation as sister in Christ, we can do it joyfully as women who have been perfectly loved and served by Christ Jesus Himself.

HYMN STANZA FOR MEDITATION

With the Lord Begin Your Task
> With the Lord begin your task;
> Jesus will direct it.
> For His aid and counsel ask;
> Jesus will perfect it.
> Ev'ry morn with Jesus rise,
> And when day is ended,
> In His name then close your eyes;
> Be to Him commended. (*LSB* 869:1)

Collect

Lord Jesus, You perfectly love us. You are patient and kind, bearing and enduring all things, even death on a cross. In You, we have eternal life, and now love truly never ends. Send us Your Spirit that we might believe all things, hope all things, and share Your perfect love with others. Amen.

LAURA

Do you not know that all of us who have been baptized into Christ Jesus were baptized into His death? We were buried therefore with Him by baptism into death, in order that, just as Christ was raised from the dead by the glory of the Father, we too might walk in newness of life. For if we have been united with Him in a death like His, we shall certainly be united with Him in a resurrection like His. We know that our old self was crucified with Him in order that the body of sin might be brought to nothing, so that we would no longer be enslaved to sin. For one who has died has been set free from sin. Now if we have died with Christ, we believe that we will also live with Him. We know that Christ, being raised from the dead, will never die again; death no longer has dominion over Him. Romans 6:3–9

Laura was heating up a snack in the break room at work when her cell phone rang.

"Hello?"

"Laura, I am on my way to pick you up." It was her husband, Dave.

"Is something wrong?"

"There are two gentleman at the house, and one is in uniform. They need to speak to you."

Laura felt her legs give out from under her. A scream escaped as she sank to the floor on her knees. Two of her three boys served in the military, one abroad and one in the states, and a home visit from an officer meant only one thing.

"Who is it?" she asked frantically as Dave helped her into the car.

"I don't know," Dave said, his face gray with unspoken worry. "They won't tell me anything as the stepfather. You are the boys' next of kin."

Laura wrung her hands in her lap, unable to sit still. She understood the need to follow military protocol, but the unknown was pure torture. "Please," she begged aloud. "Let one of them just be in trouble!"

At the house, the gentleman in uniform spoke directly to Laura. "Are you Mrs. Laura Blakely?"

"Yes," Laura answered quickly, impatient for him to continue but terrified of what he had to say.

"Mrs. Blakely, the United States Army is sad to inform you of the death of your son, Specialist Garret Porter . . ."

Laura felt the wind immediately abandon her lungs. Her stomach writhed in confusion. Garret was dead? How could her eldest son, flesh of her flesh and bone of her bones, be gone when she was still here? It wasn't supposed to happen this way. She was supposed to go first.

Later that night, Laura lay wide awake in bed, her heart heavy with unspeakable sorrow. She was not certain she could go on living in a world absent of her son.

"Stay with me, Laura," Dave whispered urgently, sensing his wife's emptiness and despair through the darkness. "Garret is with the Lord. He is the last person who needs you now. Kent, Luke, and I are the ones who need you."

Kent, Laura's middle son, called home from Fort Bragg the next morning. "Mom, I want to escort Garret's body home. My commanding officer already gave me permission."

"Are you sure?" Laura knew it was a privilege for Kent to be appointed as the escort, but she had a hard time imagining her twenty-year-old son sitting on a plane with his older brother's body stored in the cargo hold directly under his feet.

"I want to do this," Kent assured her.

A few days later, Kent dressed in uniform and saluted from the ground as Garret's flag-draped coffin was loaded onto a plane. The airline announced to the other passengers already on board that a fallen soldier was being carried on their flight and that Kent, the soldier's brother, was escorting his body home. Many of the passengers approached Kent during the flight with words of condolence. Mothers hugged him and retired military personnel shook his hand. Citizens thanked him for the sacrifices he and his brother made in service to their country. Kent had trouble swallowing several times throughout the flight, but he managed to keep his tears at bay. He would not break. His brother's final trip home would be escorted by dignity, not despair.

At the grave site, Laura wrestled with God. How could He allow her son to die? Garret still had so much life left to live. Just last week, he had called home to discuss his next move. He was months away from getting out of the army, and he wanted to come back home to go to school. He wanted to be a history teacher; he wanted to get married; he wanted to have a family. Now, he was dead, and all of his wants and desires were nothing more than chaff in the wind: blown about and gone forever. Laura hugged her youngest son, Luke, to her side, holding on for dear life.

After the funeral, Kent returned to the army base and Laura, Dave, and Luke went back to their normal lives. Yet, nothing felt normal. Garret was gone, and Laura endured a sickening wave of emptiness every time she remembered it.

"What are you thinking?" Dave asked, sitting beside his wife on their backyard swing. He took her hand in his own.

"I miss Garret."

Dave nodded. "I miss him too."

"Why did God take him away from us?"

"I've been thinking," Dave said, leaning back and looking up at the sky. "God did not take Garret away from us. God gave Garret to us for twenty-three years."

Laura sat, silently wrangling with her loss. It was difficult to reconcile Dave's words with her pain.

"Think of the gift of Garret," Dave entreated.

When Sunday morning came, Laura got up and dressed for church. She, Dave, and Luke went to Sunday School; however, when the time came for them to walk into the nave, she couldn't. She felt like a barrier was physically keeping her from entering the house of the Lord. The thought of bowing before God and singing His praises repelled her. God was the One who had allowed her son to die, and she resented Him for it. Staying away from Him was the only control she felt she had left.

"Not today," she told Dave and Luke, turning around and going home.

The next week, the same thing happened.

"What is it?" Dave asked.

"I just don't feel like going in."

"But comfort is in there."

"I don't want to be comforted," Laura's voice rattled with anger. "I want to be with my son."

Dave nodded, patiently bearing with his wife as she struggled under the weight of her grief.

"I'm jealous," Laura openly confessed, her face an open wound. "God gets to be with Garret."

"Then, let's go be with Garret too," Dave gently encouraged. "When we eat the body and drink the blood of Christ, we share the table with all the saints of heaven and earth. We share that table with Garret."

Laura walked into the church that morning as well as the next Sunday and the next. She still felt angry at God, but she was tired of fighting against the truth. Garret was with God, and she wanted to know more about his eternal life in Christ Jesus. She wanted to hear about the promise of his resurrection from the dead.

"'Do you not know that all of us who have been baptized into Christ Jesus were baptized into His death?'" Laura heard the pastor read from the Bible one Sunday morning. "'For if we have been united with Him in a death like His, we shall certainly be united with Him in a resurrection like His'" (Romans 6:3, 5).

Laura thought back to Garret's Baptism. It was then that he had been united with Christ, both in life and death. The salvation earned by Christ on the cross was his own.

"'Now if we have died with Christ,'" the pastor continued reading, "'we believe that we will also live with Him. We know that Christ, being raised from the dead, will never die again; death no longer has dominion over Him'" (Romans 6:8–9).

Christ died. But He did not stay dead. He rose, victorious over death and eternal damnation. Garret died. But because his Baptism unites him with Christ, Garret will rise again too. Laura felt the tears stream down her face. Death had no dominion over her son!

There was still more comfort to be had for Laura in church. On another Sunday, the pastor read from the Gospel of John. "'For God so loved the world, that He gave His only Son, that whoever believes in Him should not perish but have eternal life'" (John 3:16).

Laura was struck by a new thought. She had heard this verse her whole life—had memorized it as a child—yet she had never realized that God was a bereaved parent. He knew what it was like to lose a child. He really did understand her pain. In fact, He not only understood her pain of losing a child, He surpassed it. He sacrificed His child for the world.

"God loved His Son as much as I loved mine," Laura said aloud on the car ride home, "yet He willingly gave His Son up to die! I just can't imagine being that selfless."

"What do you mean?" Dave asked.

"I mean, if I had any choice in the matter, Garret would still be alive today. Can you imagine loving the world so much that you would give your son up to save it?"

"We don't have to imagine it," Dave said. "God already did it."

"Yes, He did," Laura said with true understanding, marveling at God's love for her—at God's love for Garret. God loved her son so much that He let His own Son die in Garret's place. He let Jesus take the fatal bullet of sin so that Garret might live forever. She looked out the window and smiled, her heart aglow with joy and peace. She suddenly didn't feel angry anymore. She felt thankful.

STUDY QUESTIONS

1. In Christ, is Garret really dead?

2. Romans 6 refers to our having been crucified and buried with Christ. When did we die?

3. What hope is ours now that we, in our Baptism, have died with Christ? (Romans 6:5)

4. If we, the baptized, now walk in the "newness of life" (Romans 6:4), why do we still sin?

5. If we have been united with Christ, the great Conqueror over death (Romans 6:9), why does our own flesh still perish and die?

6. In the Apostles' Creed, we confess that we believe in "the resurrection of the body, and the life everlasting." What does this mean?

7. How can Laura be thankful even when her son is dead?

_____

_____

_____

_____

_____

8. What is our hope and comfort in the face of death?

_____

_____

_____

_____

_____

A MOMENT IN THE PEW

Whenever we are given the opportunity to say something to a suffering sister in Christ, most of us tend to say the thing that would most comfort ourselves. "You'll feel better soon" or "Someday this will all make sense" or "God must have decided you are strong enough to live without your son." We try to project our own sense of order onto her chaos. We apply our own reason to her pain and explain away her loss until it can be properly labeled and filed away. Unfortunately, such remarks rarely bring comfort to our suffering sister in Christ. Her pain and grief are too present and real to be boxed up and shipped out.

It is better to let her grieve and lament, for lamentation, as we learn from King David in the Psalms, has always been a part of the Christian life. Guard your sister from your own sense of order, and let her faith, instead, respond to the Word of God. "Let the word of Christ dwell in you richly, teaching and admonishing one another in all wisdom, singing psalms and hymns and spiritual songs, with thankfulness in your hearts to God" (Colossians 3:16). Speak God's Word to your sister in Christ, listen to her, keep watch with her in her grief, pray for her, and share in her loss. Sometimes, there really is nothing for us to do but to go down into the valley and sit with those we love until our Lord sees fit to pull them out.

HYMN STANZA FOR MEDITATION

No Saint on Earth Lives Life to Self Alone
No saint on earth lives life to self alone
Or dies alone, for we with Christ are one.
So if we live, for Christ alone we live,
And if we die, to Christ our dying give.
In living and in dying this confess:
We are the Lord's, safe in God's faithfulness.
(*LSB* 747:1)

Collect

Lord God, You know the sting of death. You forsook
Your own beloved Child on the cross that we might
live forever as Your dear children. Do not abandon us
to the grave, but, just as You raised Your Son from the
dead, make us to hear Your trumpet call on the Last
Day and wake us in the flesh to spend eternity with
You. Through Jesus Christ, Your Son, our risen Lord and
Savior. Amen.

HOPE

I will bless the LORD at all times;
>   His praise shall continually be in my mouth.

My soul makes its boast in the LORD;
>   let the humble hear and be glad.

Oh, magnify the LORD with me,
>   and let us exalt His name together!

I sought the LORD, and He answered me
>   and delivered me from all my fears.

Those who look to Him are radiant,
>   and their faces shall never be ashamed.

This poor man cried, and the LORD heard him
>   and saved him out of all his troubles.

The angel of the LORD encamps
>   around those who fear Him, and delivers them.

Oh, taste and see that the LORD is good!
>   Blessed is the man who takes refuge in Him!

Oh, fear the LORD, you His saints,
>   for those who fear Him have no lack!

The young lions suffer want and hunger;
>   but those who seek the LORD lack no good thing.

Come, O children, listen to me;
>   I will teach you the fear of the LORD.

What man is there who desires life
　　and loves many days, that he may see good?
Keep your tongue from evil
　　and your lips from speaking deceit.
Turn away from evil and do good;
　　seek peace and pursue it.
The eyes of the LORD are toward the righteous
　　and His ears toward their cry.
The face of the LORD is against those who do evil,
　　to cut off the memory of them from the earth.
When the righteous cry for help, the LORD hears
　　and delivers them out of all their troubles.
The LORD is near to the brokenhearted
　　and saves the crushed in spirit.
Many are the afflictions of the righteous,
　　but the LORD delivers him out of them all.

Psalm 34:1–19

Hope sat down in a pew on the pulpit side of the nave. She felt a little bit like an immigrant in a foreign land. The balcony was her native home, and the choir was her tribe. For over thirty-five years she had lived in the alto section, faithfully proclaiming the Word in song to her neighbors below, but circumstances had necessitated a deportation downstairs away from the melismata and arpeggios. Her singing voice, once rich and lush in tone, now cracked and wavered with every breath.

Hope first noticed a change when driving home from her niece's wedding. The symptoms came on quickly: a sore throat followed by a cough, then a raging fever with aches. She tried to convince herself that it was nothing more than just a bad cold, but one swab of the back of her throat was all her doctor needed to confirm the dreaded truth: swine flu.

Hope holed up in her home, miserable with fatigue. She could barely move for the muscle aches, but her congestion was the worst. She coughed and coughed to clear her throat, trying in vain to move the stubborn phlegm from her vocal chords. A thick blanket of mucus dampened her voice, restricting the chords from vibrating and producing any sound. Even when her flu symptoms faded, her voice remained hoarse and raspy. She opened her mouth to sing, but the song that came out sounded more like a strangled cat than a grown woman.

Fearing the worst, Hope made an appointment with an ear, nose, and throat doctor.

"I don't see any permanent damage," the ENT reassured, studying the digital image projected from the scope. "I do, however, see a light coating of mucus clinging to your chords. Perhaps gastric reflux is the culprit. I'll write you a prescription that should clear it up."

Hope obediently took her medication, and, a couple of months later, she did notice a difference. Her voice remained strangely feline, but it had regained a fraction of its previous strength and endurance. As long as she stuck to the low notes, she could actually sustain a pitch without breaking. Perhaps she was ready to climb back out of the alley and onto the balcony again. Hesitantly, Hope returned to choir practice.

"Hope's back!" the director called out with glee as Hope walked through the door. It had been two months since she had joined in on a rehearsal, and the room erupted with cheers and applause.

"Don't you dare think of leaving us ever again," Martha

threatened, tightly hugging Hope around the neck. "We altos are lost without you."

Truth be told, Hope had been lost without them. The choir was her family, and she had been homesick for their harmonious company. She felt such relief to be back in the choir where she belonged. She picked up her music folder and sighed with contentment. Her musical reprieve, however, was short-lived. Her voice soon failed her again, only this time it abandoned her immediately following a knee-replacement surgery.

"I don't get it," Martha said, sitting bedside in the hospital. "How could knee surgery possibly hurt your voice?"

"I don't know," Hope whispered, her words all air and no resonance. Her throat felt fine, but her voice was completely empty of sound. She trekked back to the ENT's office.

"Your left vocal chord appears to be paralyzed," he said.

"Why?" Hope mouthed.

"I'm not sure. Nothing showed up on your sonogram or x-rays. Maybe it's a virus?"

Hope felt defeated. Losing her voice once was bad enough, but twice? In the same year? How could she possibly hope to recover when a specialist couldn't even figure out how to fix it? Fearing her balcony days were over, Hope resigned herself to the nave. She sat with the rest of the congregation, listening as the choir cantered the Gradual and belted the Offertory from the balcony. She tried to feel grateful to be on the receiving end of such musical delights, but it killed her not to be up there singing herself. She picked up a hymnal and silently followed along during the service while her pew mates sang the liturgical responses and hymns. Every cell in her body rebelled at not being able to join her voice in song with the people of God. She felt like the prayers of the church had been stolen right out from under her along with her voice.

Hope tried opening one more door. She made an appointment with an otolaryngologist, a doctor who specialized in the diagnosis and correction of vocal problems. If this doctor couldn't help recover her voice, no one could.

"It is indeed a paralyzed vocal chord," the specialist confirmed, "but I see no irritation in the nerve. The only thing I can think is that your left chord may have experienced trauma from intubation during your knee surgery. Since the paralyzed chord is no longer moving to meet up with the functioning chord, you can't phonate. I am going to try to plump the paralyzed chord up with injections. Perhaps moving it closer to the functioning chord will help you achieve sound."

Perhaps? Hope went home to ponder her plight. Since the age of five, she had been singing in church. What would she do if the injections didn't work? What if the rest of her life was a perpetual Lent, void of Easter alleluias and Christmas glorias? What if she never got to sing "The Lord's Prayer" at another wedding? What was her life without the gift of song?

Martha sought Hope out in the narthex after church the next Sunday.

"It's official," Martha announced. "Katy is getting married this summer."

Hope's eyes teared up with both joy and sadness. She was happy to hear of her goddaughter's betrothal, but she also knew her voice most likely would not be ready by then to sing "The Lord's Prayer" for Katy's wedding. She had always dreamed of doing that for her goddaughter.

"I know what you're thinking," Martha said, gripping

Hope's arm to give her strength, "and we've already made a decision. If you can't sing in Katy's wedding, then we don't want anyone to sing."

The tears rolled freely down Hope's cheeks.

"You are what is important," Martha continued, "We love your voice, but we love you even more. As long as you are there, that is all that matters."

After Martha left, Hope lingered in the narthex to consider what her friend had just said. *She* was what was important? Hope had always assumed that music was what made her unique. Singing had always been her special talent, her God-given gift to share with others, and losing it had made her feel confused about who she was to her family, friends, and the church. What could she possibly give to her brothers and sisters in Christ now that she had no voice? What could she contribute to her goddaughter's wedding if not the gift of song?

Hope went to Katy's wedding, and she sat in the nave with all of the other guests. When the time came for the Lord's Prayer, Hope bowed her head and silently added her voice to the congregation's in petitioning that God's will be done in the life of her goddaughter and of the whole Body of Christ. She was not able to sing the words as she had originally dreamed, but her prayer was heard just the same. That, Hope realized, was a gift far more precious than any song she could ever sing, and it was one no flu episode or surgery could ever take away. Her prayers, even the silent ones, would be heard by her Father in heaven, and she could pray anywhere, at any time, with or without a voice.

Hope still keeps her prayers coming today, though she prefers to sing them. Those injections worked, after all.

STUDY QUESTIONS

1. Hope lost her voice. There are times when we are made mute in our grief and pain. How can we know with assurance that God still hears our prayers even when we cannot speak? (Romans 8:26–28)

2. Does God always answer our prayers?

3. The psalmist writes that "those who seek the LORD lack no good thing" (Psalm 34:10). Does this mean that God will give us everything we want when we pray to Him?

4. What does God promise for the righteous who pray?

5. How should we pray?

6. What can you do to help the young in your church memorize the Lord's Prayer?

7. The psalmist urges us to "taste and see that the LORD is good!" (Psalm 34:8). Where in the Divine Service are we given opportunity to do this?

8. God's good gifts of Word and Sacrament are given
   for the benefit of all in the Body of Christ, not just
   those who can speak, see, hear, and move. What are
   ways we can help the mute, blind, deaf, and lame
   receive those good gifts in church?

   ....

   ....

   ....

   ....

   ....

   ....

A MOMENT IN THE PEW

Have you ever lost your voice? Maybe you have never had vocal trouble such as Hope, but have you ever felt your voice catch in your throat at the sight of a particular word in the hymnal or at the sound of the opening melody of a beloved hymn? Maybe you unexpectedly hear the hymn that was sung at your mother's funeral or come across a poetic line in stanza 3 that beams Christ's light of hope into your weary heart.

Whatever the reason, it happens sometimes. You take a deep breath, and your diaphragm rubs up against a forgotten ball of grief buried deep inside your gut. Your stomach recoils, shuddering all music-making air out of your lungs. You try to sing anyway, but your throat constricts and holds your larynx in a vise grip. Next, your eyes betray you, blurring the words on the page with tears.

You may find yourself temporarily struck mute and blind in church, but you are not left forsaken in the pew. The Word still prevails through the mouths of your song-preaching neighbors. Their voices sing loud and clear for your benefit, proclaiming the Word in song to you when you are struck silent in your grief. So, sing out and sing loud, my sisters! You never know when someone sitting before, behind, or beside you might be in need of it.

HYMN STANZA FOR MEDITATION

Our Father, Who from Heaven Above

> Our Father, who from heav'n above
> Bids all of us to live in love
> As members of one family
> And pray to You in unity,
> Teach us no thoughtless words to say
> But from our inmost hearts to pray.
> (*LSB* 766:1)

Collect

Our Father who art in heaven, hallowed be Thy name, Thy kingdom come, Thy will be done on earth as it is in heaven. Give us this day our daily bread; and forgive us our trespasses as we forgive those who trespass against us; and lead us not into temptation, but deliver us from evil. For Thine is the kingdom and the power and the glory forever and ever. Amen.

GABRIELLA

Behold, children are a heritage from the LORD,
 the fruit of the womb a reward.
Like arrows in the hand of a warrior
 are the children of one's youth.
Blessed is the man
 who fills his quiver with them!
He shall not be put to shame
 when he speaks with his enemies in the gate.
Psalm 127:3–5

Gabriella felt a bit off in that familiar kind of way.

"It can't be," Simon assured her. "Ben is only five months old. It's too soon."

It was early, even for them, but Gabriella felt almost certain. She took a pregnancy test the next morning just to be sure.

"I think it's positive," Simon squinted at the plastic stick resting on the bathroom counter. "The line is faint, but it's definitely there."

Gabriella closed her eyes in silent resignation.

"We're pregnant," Simon grinned, laughing nervously. He

turned around to share the joy with his wife, but Gabriella wasn't laughing. She was crying.

"It's going to be okay," Simon soothed, taking his wife in his arms.

Gabriella took a shaky breath.

"We can do this," Simon comforted.

Gabriella wasn't so sure.

"Just think," Simon marveled. "Baby number six!"

At that, Gabriella spurted out a laugh. She couldn't help it. The number sounded so ridiculous.

Later that morning, Gabriella fought back tears of contrition as she nursed little Ben. She caressed his soft, pink cheeks and listened to the gentle hum of his suckling. Just five months before she had given birth to this precious baby boy, and now he was no longer the baby of the family. Like all of his older siblings, he would have to grow up so quickly. His roly-poly legs would need to walk independently by his first birthday, and shortly after that he would need to learn to put on his own shoes and coat. First, though, Ben would need to learn that mommy's lap was for sharing. A stab of guilt pierced through Gabriella's heart.

That was not Gabriella's only grief. Later in the day, when all of the kids were happily occupied with books, puzzles, and baby dolls, Gabriella snuck down to the basement and closed the bathroom door. She stepped on the scale and stared at the number. She was just seven pounds shy of her postpartum goal weight, but, now that she was pregnant, she would never meet it. She cried out loud, her bitter disappointment rolling down her cheeks in streams.

"I don't think I can take care of another person," Gabriella confessed to Simon later that night before bed. "I just figured out how to care for five children. How in the world am I going to care for six?"

Simon put down the book he was reading and looked at his wife.

"I mean, I just now feel like myself again, like I can somewhat successfully take care of you and the kids and the house without being a zombie, and now, well . . . now it's going to start all over again."

"What's going to start?"

Gabriella felt her throat tighten and her eyes sting. "The looks and the comments. People already think I'm a freak. I can see them doing the math in their heads whenever they look at me and the kids. They're going to think I'm a baby hoarder when they find out I'm pregnant with a sixth."

"Those same people would think you were a baby hater if you weren't pregnant. They're just looking for something to criticize."

Gabriella blew her nose. "I just get so tired of being misunderstood."

"I know," Simon sighed. "People at work tell me that I have a rich man's family, that I have double the right amount of children."

"What do you say to them?"

Simon shrugged. "In some ways I can't argue with them. I am rich, though not in the way they mean. I am rich with God's gift of children. Six times rich!"

Gabriella smiled for the first time that day.

"You know," Simon continued, "if it was any other gift from God—money, possessions, health, whatever—people would welcome it without question. They would even ask God for more of it. No one would ever dare to think that God was giving them too much money or too big of a house, and they would never think of turning those gifts away. So, why do we not welcome the gift of children in the same way, especially when God tells us in His Word that they are a gift?"

Gabriella moved closer to her husband and leaned against his arm.

"I know you're tired," Simon kissed Gabriella's forehead, "and it's probably going to get worse in the next few months. How can I help you?"

"You already did." Gabriella turned out the light. She knew exactly what to pray for that night and every night after. "Lord, help me to see the child you are giving me as a gift."

Several weeks later, Gabriella and Simon decided to tell the kids.

"We're having a baby," Simon announced.

"Noooo," five-year-old Paul grinned, certain he had caught his parents midtease. He pointed to Ben resting in his mother's arms. "We have a baby, right here."

"There's another baby," Simon said.

"Where?" Chloe asked.

"In my tummy," Gabriella explained, "but the baby's still growing."

Little Miriam stared wide-eyed at her mommy's belly, utterly confused.

"Really?" John, the eldest, asked.

"Really," Simon confirmed.

John beamed with pride and delight. As far as he was concerned, the baby was as good as his. Paul and Chloe jumped up and down and yelled with excitement, and Miriam stood protectively in front of Baby Ben to shield him from all the noise. Simon grinned at his wife, and Gabriella smiled with joy. The kids understood. They got it. This baby really was a gift.

Chloe could barely contain her excitement for this new gift. On Sunday, she raised her hand during the children's sermon and proudly announced, "My mommy is having a baby in her tummy."

Gabriella wanted to sink into the floor. Simon shrugged and smiled as if to say, "What can you do?"

There were no congratulations offered after church. No well-wishers stopped by to give their compliments. Only quick glances and guarded smiles were thrown over shoulders eager to get away.

Out in the narthex, one woman boldly approached Gabriella and looked her squarely in the eye. "Are you really pregnant?"

"Yes." Gabriella's cheeks burned, hoping the children weren't listening.

"Wow. Really?"

Surely this woman's question was rhetorical. Gabriella remained silent and looked around for Simon. He was busily engaged in conversation with one of the ushers several feet away.

"You must be busy!" The woman's eyes contained all of the necessary subtext.

Gabriella noticed John's head cock to the side as he tried to figure out what the woman meant. The woman noticed too.

"Tell me, young man. How old are you?"

"I am seven."

The woman glanced around at John and his siblings, quickly doing the math. Finally, she rested her accusing gaze on Gabriella. "Do you always need to have an infant in your arms?"

Gabriella felt the anger, the injustice of this woman's insinuations, rising to a fever pitch. Should she say something or not? Would this woman even listen?

"I'm not addicted to babies, if that's what you mean." Gabriella's quiet voice shook with emotion. She willed herself not to cry. *Not here. Not now. Not in front of the kids.* "And I don't think I'm a supermom or anything. Most days, I feel anything but super." Deep breath. "I am just trying to receive with joy the gifts God wants to give me."

There. She had said it. She did not wait to see how the woman reacted but quickly pulled her kids out to the parking lot. They would all wait for Simon in the van; but, before she could finish buckling Miriam into her car seat, Gabriella heard another woman's voice speak to her from behind.

"Um, excuse me."

Gabriella turned around, afraid.

"Oh, I'm sorry to bother you." The woman looked nervous. "I just wanted to say—I mean, I wanted to catch you before you left."

Gabriella stood still, waiting for it.

"You are Chloe's mother, right?"

Gabriella nodded yes.

"I substituted for Chloe's Sunday School class this morning, and she told me that you are expecting. It is wonderful news!

And if your baby turns out to be anything like Chloe, well then, what a delight!"

Gabriella remembered this woman now. She sat on the pulpit side of the church toward the back with her husband. Gabriella had never seen them with any children.

"Anyway, I just wanted to tell you congratulations."

"Oh, thank you!" Gabriella snapped out of her stupor. "My name is Gabriella."

"I'm Molly," the woman smiled warmly.

"Hi, Miss Molly!" Chloe called from deep within the recesses of the van.

"Hi, Chloe," Molly waved through the van window. "Don't forget to practice your Baptism song this week."

"I won't, Miss Molly!"

Gabriella watched as Molly chatted back and forth with each of the children. She even stuck her head through the door to coo at Ben. When she turned back around to face Gabriella, her eyes were glistening with joy and sorrow.

"Children are such a gift, aren't they?" Molly asked.

In that moment, Gabriella realized that God had answered her prayer. Through the eyes of Molly, she could now fully see the generosity of God's good gifts to her and Simon.

"Yes," she answered. "Yes, they are."

STUDY QUESTIONS

1. What does God's Word tell us that children are to us?

2. Does God will for children to be the good fruit of the one-flesh union in marriage? (Genesis 1:27–28)

3. What things in life tempt us to avoid the gift of children in marriage? Is it ever okay to avoid the gift of children in marriage?

4. Is God punishing marriages when He withholds the gift of children from them? Why are some married couples barren?

5. Mary's response to the news of her pregnancy is "Behold, I am the servant of the Lord; let it be to me according to your word" (Luke 1:38). What can we learn from Mary's example?

6. Will God always provide the means for us to care for the children that He gives us? How can we be sure? (Matthew 6:25–34; Romans 8:32)

7. As Christians, what are our responsibilities in rearing the children God gives to us? (Ephesians 6:4) How can married couples who have not been given the gift of children be parents in the Church?

----

8. Jesus bids us to let the little children come to Him. How do we do this? (Matthew 19:14–15)

A MOMENT IN THE PEW

It can be hard not to judge others for the size of their family. After all, the world encourages us to pass judgment by its language alone: "family planning, stewardship, baby machine, reproduction, fertility science, selective termination, abortion." All of these worldly terms suggest children to be a commodity—a consumer product—to be planned for, made, controlled, and even rejected. Yet, we Christians know that God calls children something very different in His Word, "heritage, blessing, fruit, reward," and we know what to do with His blessings. We are to welcome them in faith, celebrate, and rejoice in them.

The next time you sit down in your pew and look around at your brothers and sisters in Christ, try not to speculate whether or not they have too many or too few gifts from God. Instead, thank God that He gives gifts to all of us, and pray that He will help us to know and trust that His gifts are good.

HYMN STANZAS FOR MEDITATION

How Clear Is Our Vocation, Lord

How clear is our vocation, Lord,
When once we heed Your call:
To live according to Your Word
And daily learn, refreshed, restored,
That You are Lord of all
And will not let us fall.

In what You give us, Lord, to do,
Together or alone,
In old routines or ventures new,
May we not cease to look to You,
The cross You hung upon—
All You endeavored done. (*LSB* 853:1, 3)

Collect

Heavenly Father, You give us such good gifts. Help us
to receive those gifts with thankfulness and joy, knowing them to be an extension of Your steadfast love and
tender care for us; through Jesus Christ, Your Son, our
Lord, who lives and reigns with You and the Holy Spirit,
one God, now and forever. Amen.

Session Eleven

CHRISTINE

Who shall separate us from the love of Christ? Shall tribulation, or distress, or persecution, or famine, or nakedness, or danger, or sword? As it is written, "For Your sake we are being killed all the day long; we are regarded as sheep to be slaughtered." No, in all these things we are more than conquerors through Him who loved us. For I am sure that neither death nor life, nor angels nor rulers, nor things present nor things to come, nor powers, nor height nor depth, nor anything else in all creation, will be able to separate us from the love of God in Christ Jesus our Lord. Romans 8:35–39

Christine was doing good things in her life. She faithfully took care of her husband and two children, served her church as the head of Sunday School, and volunteered as co-chair of the school auction. She was good to life, and life was good to her. That is why the bad news came like a punch to the gut.

"We found something in your sonogram yesterday," Christine's ob-gyn told her over the phone one Wednesday morning while Christine was dropping her kids off at school. "I don't know what it is. I need you to get a CT scan."

Christine went in for a scan the very next day, and the results called for immediate action. "You definitely need surgery, so we want you to meet with an oncologist tomorrow."

An oncologist? Christine was frozen with fear.

"I'm not sure what this is," the oncologist said in a consultation the following day. "We'll start with a laparoscopy. If it looks bad, I'll open you up and take it out."

How could this be happening? Christine was a faithful servant of her church. Wouldn't God protect her after all of the good works she had done?

The oncologist broke the news as soon as Christine woke from surgery. "You have Stage III ovarian cancer. It left the pelvic area and was also in the abdomen. I think I removed all of it, but you were in surgery for hours."

Cancer. Christine's greatest fear had materialized. For hours she wept, causing massive physical pain to emanate from her post-surgery abdomen. The unknown was terrifying. What would happen to her family? Who would care for her children? "Please, don't let me die. Please, don't let me die . . ." Christine prayed over and over again.

Tests were done. Specialists were consulted. Chemotherapy began, and Christine had to stop all of her previous activities. The subsequent fatigue and bone pain in her legs were almost more than she could bear. She could no longer participate in all of her children's school functions, and guilt became her steady companion during the long hours of each pain-filled day. What had she done to deserve all of this?

"Why is this happening?" Christine demanded of her pastor.

"Sin is why this is happening. Sin brought all of this suffering into the world," he answered.

Christine began examining her life, searching desperately for any sin she may have committed that would warrant such a curse as cancer. If she could somehow figure out what she had done to deserve this punishment from God, then maybe she could figure out a way to earn God's favor back again. Maybe she could control this disease, after all.

"I do not mean any particular sin of your own, Christine," Pastor continued, "but the sin of all mankind. When Adam and Eve first broke God's command and ate from the tree of the knowledge of good and evil, sin entered the world. Now, all of creation groans in response to it, and illnesses, such as cancer, attack our bodies. Sin is what causes this pain and suffering. But, Christine, I have Good News: your sin has been taken away by Jesus' death on the cross!"

"Does that mean Jesus will take away my cancer too?"

"I pray that He will," Pastor leaned forward and looked Christine in the eye. "However, I cannot promise that you are going to survive this temporal disease. I cannot promise that you will be here to see your children a year from now. I cannot even promise that I will be here to shepherd them, for none of us is promised tomorrow. What I can promise you is that God has, in Christ, healed you from the disease of sin and will keep you alive with Him forever."

"But, I want to live *now*." Christine looked down at her hands. "I don't know what I did to deserve this."

"You are barking up the wrong tree, Christine. You are looking for there to be a consequence to the action of your sin, but there is none. You are God's child, and He does not punish you for your sin. He already punished Christ in your place. It is true that apart from Christ we all deserve death, but you are not apart from Christ. You are baptized into His name, and now you share in the gifts of salvation He has won for you on the cross."

"If God does not punish His children, then why is this happening to me?" Christine cried.

"Just as you share in the gifts of Christ, you also share in the suffering of Christ. Jesus suffered, so we can expect to suffer too. God's Word does not tell us exactly how. It will be different for each of us, yet even in the face of something as terrible and horrible as cancer God promises that neither height nor depth nor even death will be able to separate you from His love in Christ Jesus."

"I don't want to suffer," Christine confided. "I have tried so hard to be good, to do what God and everyone expects of me. This is not supposed to happen to people who do good."

"That is what the world tells you. Nowhere does God say in His Word that doing good works earn us His favor. Quite the contrary, God's Word says that His favor is ours as a gift because of Jesus. Just as pain and suffering in this life are not signs of God's anger toward you, health and happiness are not signs of God's favor."

"I am afraid to do anything good anymore for fear that this will all happen again," Christine whispered.

Pastor's voice was tender. "I can understand your fear. This all came as a sucker punch, didn't it? Even if you survive this cancer, what's to say this won't all happen again? But, Christine, I promise you that all of this is happening outside of whatever good or bad things you have done. It's just happening, and we can't exactly know why it's happening to you." Pastor took a deep breath. "Whatever happens in this life, though, you can be certain of one thing: your Redeemer lives, and at the Last Day He will stand upon the earth. And after your skin has been thus destroyed, yet in your flesh you will see God!"

STUDY QUESTIONS

1. In what ways do you suffer in this life?

----

2. Christine wonders if her own suffering is a punishment from God for her personal sins. Some sins do indeed have physical consequences in this world (such as STDs resulting from fornication or incarceration resulting from breaking civil law), but why does God not punish you, His child, for your personal sins?

----

3. How do you know with certainty that you are a child of God? (Galatians 3:26–29; 4:4–7) What promises does God give you as His child and heir? (Romans 6:3–5)

4. Is any one of us "good"? (Galatians 3:10; Ephesians 2:1–3) What makes us good in the eyes of God? (Acts 2:38–39; 1 Corinthians 6:11; Titus 3:4–7)

5. Do good works earn God's favor? (Ephesians 2:4–9) As Christians, why do we do good works? (Romans 6:17–19; Ephesians 2:10; Titus 3:8)

6. What is the irony of calling someone a "good" Christian?

_____

_____

_____

_____

_____

7. Why can we expect to suffer in this life, even though we do good works? (Philippians 3:7–11; 1 Peter 4:12–19) What sure comfort do we have in the face of suffering? (2 Corinthians 12:9–10)

_____

_____

_____

_____

8. What is Christine's true victory over cancer?

_____

_____

_____

_____

A MOMENT IN THE PEW

Cancer is the scariest of villains. It is a caped grim reaper that hides in the dark and attacks when its victim least expects. It fights to the death, and it shows no mercy. That is why we are afraid. We know cancer cares nothing for our life, our family, our friends, our work, or even our happiness. It cares only for its own survival.

Do you know of a sister in Christ who is currently battling cancer? Does she live alone, or does she have a family? What can you do to help her? Certainly you can pray for her and petition that God, should it be according to His perfect will, bring her back to full health and vitality, but you can also take care of her physical needs. You can make sure she and her family have meals to eat; you can give her children rides home from soccer practice and see to it that they have proper care while their mom is ill; you can make sure everyone has a way to get to church on Sundays to receive Christ's gifts of Word and Sacrament, and, if your sister in Christ is unable to leave her hospital or home, you can make sure your pastor is aware of her need for a visit; you can visit her in the hospital yourself; and you can sit by her bed and read to her to help take her mind off of the pain. Whatever it is you can do for your sister in Christ, it can be done in faith that God loves and cares for her in Jesus even while she has cancer.

The Will of God Is Always Best

> When life's brief course on earth is run
> And I this world am leaving,
> Grant me to say, "Your will be done,"
> Your faithful Word believing.
> My dearest Friend, I now commend
> My soul into Your keeping;
> From sin and hell, And death as well,
> By You the vict'ry reaping. (*LSB* 758:4)

Collect

Blessed Lord, You joined us to Your Son in the waters of Holy Baptism, making His righteousness our own. Death no longer has dominion over any of us in Christ Jesus though we still suffer from disease in this world. Comfort us amidst these earthly trials, helping us to trust that just as Christ was raised from the dead, so, too, will our bodies be raised on the Resurrection Day; through Jesus Christ, Your Son, our Lord, who lives and reigns with You and the Holy Spirit, one God, now and forever. Amen.

Session Twelve

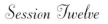

EVE

It is in vain that you rise up early
and go late to rest,
eating the bread of anxious toil;
for He gives to His beloved sleep.

Psalm 127:2

Eve felt like a floppy fish in bed. She tossed back and forth from side to front to side and then flat on her back again. It was the middle of the night, but her mind raced as if it was still high noon. Conversations from the previous day played over and over again in her head.

"My co-worker is pregnant," Johanna had confided over the phone earlier that evening. "That's seven, Mom. I now have seven friends who are all pregnant."

Eve's heart broke for her daughter.

"When will it be my turn?" Johanna cried.

Lord, have mercy! Eve silently prayed.

"I am the only one left of all of my friends who isn't a mother," Johanna's voice twisted as if it was being wrung out like a wet dishrag.

Eve wished she could somehow reach through the phone line and wrap her daughter in her arms like she had back when Johanna was a little girl. They could snuggle in the rocking chair again, Johanna nestling her blankie and Eve singing "I Am Jesus' Little Lamb," and forget about all of the pain and disappointment of the adult world.

"Mom," Johanna whispered through her tears, "what if I never become a mother?"

Eve felt her daughter's pain as if it was her own. She wanted so desperately to offer some kind of advice that would magically turn Johanna's pumpkin into a happily-ever-after ending. She wanted to make promises of children and car seats and happiness in the future, but, deep down inside, Eve knew that Johanna would see straight through all of the colored smoke to the black-and-white of reality. No, Johanna needed the unconditional love and acceptance of her mother, not a fairy tale. "I love you, Johanna. I am already so proud of you, mother or not. You are a faithful wife to Jacob, a favorite aunt to Marin and Mark, and a beloved teacher to hundreds of school kids. Whatever happens, whatever God has in store for you and Jacob as a family, you are the most beautiful daughter in the world. I love you just the way you are."

Eve returned to the darkness of her bedroom and flipped over onto her side. The electric blue numbers of the alarm clock beamed a bright 3:28. Only four minutes had passed. Why did time always stand still in the middle of the night? Eve willed herself to fall asleep, but her mind restlessly jumped to Peter's call from earlier that evening.

"I didn't get the job, Mom," Peter had sighed into the phone.

Eve fought back a sigh of her own. Just seven months earlier, Peter had been laid off of his teaching job after fifteen years of faithful service to the school district, and no other school in this economy seemed interested in hiring a teacher with his extensive education and years of experience.

"The superintendent hired a girl right out of college," Peter explained, his voice tight with stress. "I wasn't even considered."

"But you subbed at that school for four months," Eve spurted out the words before she could stop them. "The department head said you were his first choice."

"The department head didn't even have a say in the decision," Peter said. "The superintendent hired over his head."

Lord, have mercy! Eve silently prayed, again.

"Well, Mom, I need to put the kids in bed. Mark has little league practice in the morning, and Marin has cheer camp. I just wanted you to know."

Eve bit her lip, trying to think of something to say, some comfort to offer her only son. She flashed back to a time years ago when Peter had rushed to her with his little arms outstretched, his rosy cheeks glistening with bright, shiny tears, and his right knee all scuffed and bruised from a sidewalk spill on his roller skates. She had been able to make everything better then with just a kiss and a bandage, but there were no easy bandages or salves for this kind of wound.

"I love you, Peter," Eve said, careful to keep her voice bright and sincere. Pity would do him no good. "I am praying for you. Just let me know if you want me and your father to take the kids this weekend. You and Kerry might like some time to yourselves before the school year starts again."

Eve gritted her teeth and stared at the ripple of shadows cast by the moonlight shining across her spackled bedroom ceiling. She knew her children had to bear their own burdens, but it was so hard not to worry. She had always been a Martha, eager to serve her family with her hands. She was much more comfortable doing something rather than just being, but, now that her children were grown, they needed her to be more of a Mary these days. What else could she do but listen, watch, and pray?

Eve's mind flitted back to her visit with her parents the day before.

"He's getting more anxious," Eve's mother had disclosed after lunch. "He wants to help with the farming, but he can barely walk."

Eve looked across the room at her aging father. He sat in a cushioned chair by the window, restlessly watching a baler at work in a hayfield north of the house. His ankles, swollen from years of battling high blood sugar and hypertension, were propped up on an ottoman. Eve fought back tears of sadness. Her father had always been a hard worker and a faithful provider for his family, and it pained her to see him so cruelly grounded by aching hips and failing knees.

"Is he still using the walker?"

Eve's mother nodded yes, but they both knew it would not be long before her father's fickle balance would further confine him to a wheelchair.

"He insists on driving," Eve's mother whispered. "Just yesterday, he got the truck out and drove it into town."

"Can't you drive for him, Mom?"

She shook her head. "He won't even hear of it."

Eve knew what she had to do, but the task set before her was as wretched and unsavory as anything she had ever encountered. How could she presume to parent her own father? Yet, it was too dangerous for him to drive in his present condition. *Lord, have mercy!* her heart cried. She took a deep breath and looked her mother in the eye. "I think we are going to have to take away his keys."

Eve's stomach churned at the memory. She watched as the shadow of a hard maple growing outside her bedroom window traveled slowly down the west wall. Soon, the moon would set, and her bedroom would be in total darkness like her thoughts. She was weary of wrestling with her memories. Not one moment of this invisible struggle would add a single hour to her life nor to the lives of her loved ones, yet the enemy was persistent in his attack. He did not wage war according to the flesh, but struck her knowledge of God with arrows of anxiety and pierced her faith in God's promises with spears of doubt. She would need divine artillery to destroy her opponent's strongholds.

"'Humble yourselves,'" Eve whispered, raising the hefty shield of the Word of God, "'casting all your anxieties on Him, because He cares for you'" (1 Peter 5:7). There was no need to worry about her children. God promised to provide for their daily bread, and He would do just that.

"'We know that for those who love God all things work together for good'" (Romans 8:28). Eve struck deep at the heart of her enemy with the sword of the Holy Spirit. She did not need to fear for her father. God promised, in Jesus, to never fail him in life or in death.

"'In peace I will both lie down and sleep,'" Eve closed her eyes, fastening on the belt of truth, "'for You alone, O LORD, make me dwell in safety'" (Psalm 4:8).

Eve pictured the face of her Savior. He would keep her through the night; He would make her dwell in safety; He would shoulder her burdens; He would . . .

STUDY QUESTIONS

1. What keeps you awake at night?

2. What are we to do with our worries, cares, and anxious toiling? (1 Peter 5:7)

3. How can we effectively combat those demons which torment us in the sleepless hours of the night? (Ephesians 6:10–18)

_____

_____

_____

_____

4. We, like Eve, can't help but want to fix the problems
of those we love. How can we best serve our loved
ones who suffer? How is Eve's prayer, "Lord, have
mercy," a good one?

_____

_____

_____

_____

5. Eve put her "Martha" skills to good use when raising
her young children: changing diapers, cooking, clean-
ing, schooling, shopping, carpooling, you name it.
What kinds of "Mary" skills will be helpful to her in
parenting her adult children? (Luke 10:38–42)

_____

_____

_____

6. Eve found herself in the difficult situation of needing
to parent her own parent. Is she breaking the Fourth
Commandment of our Lord, "Honor your father
and your mother," when she acts against her father's
wishes? (Exodus 20:12)

7. How do we help, serve, and protect our aging parents, all the while still honoring them?

8. Sometimes, it is not the spirit but the body which keeps us awake at night. Hormone changes, metabolic shifts, and even a late-night cup of coffee can steal our precious sleep. What are some worthy things we can do in those restless hours?

A MOMENT IN THE PEW

Thank God for Marthas! Where would we be in the Church today without our ladies aid societies, altar guilds, sewing circles, office staff, Sunday School teachers, or funeral luncheon committees? We would definitely be less organized and more hungry, and our pastors would most certainly be underserved. It is a good thing to use our hands to take care of the needs of our pastor and the church, just as it was a good thing for Martha to use her hands to care for the physical needs of Jesus and His disciples.

Still, we need to be Marys and "choose the good portion." We come to church, not to serve, but to be served by Jesus. As much as we like to busy our hands with this task and that piece of work for the benefit of our Lord, it is good, right, and salutary that we should sit at the Lord's feet and listen to His teaching. So, do not neglect your good portion. Come to church and hear your pastor preach the Word to you in the Lord's name. Eat Christ's body and drink His blood for your salvation. Receive His blessing with thanksgiving, and then, as you get up to leave, get those Martha-hands ready. Someone is going to need you to do the dishes.

HYMN STANZA FOR MEDITATION

God, Who Made the Earth and Heaven

> God, who made the earth and heaven,
> Darkness and light:
> You the day for work have given,
> For rest the night.
> May Your angel guards defend us,
> Slumber sweet Your mercy send us,
> Holy dreams and hopes attend us
> All through the night. (*LSB* 877:1)

Collect

Heavenly Father, You promise to give us, Your beloved, sleep. In the anxious hours of the morning, when we are alone in the dark and tempted by the devil's schemes, help us to trust in Your certain promise to bear our burdens and to make us ever dwell in safety; through Jesus Christ, Your Son, our Lord, who lives and reigns with You and the Holy Spirit, one God, now and forever. Amen.

STUDY GUIDE

When it comes to the application of God's Word, I am really good at asking questions, but I am not so good at coming up with answers; or, to be more exact, I do not trust myself to properly interpret Scripture in its truth and purity. I have never studied Greek or Hebrew, and I have no formal training in exegetical studies. While I have skills in analyzing literature in the English language, I do not fool myself into believing that a single, published, English translation of the Bible perfectly communicates the grammar and syntax of antiquity's languages. For this reason, I go to my pastors with my questions about the Bible. They have studied God's Word in its original languages, and, most important, they have been called by God to preach and teach it to me in its truth and purity. Now, that's a brand I can trust.

In this study guide, you will find answers for each of the study questions in this book. I asked my own pastors, Rev. Brent McGuire and Rev. Michael Schuermann, these questions, and the answers provided below are transcripts of what they told me. I hope you will find their responses helpful, and, as you chew on these truths and ponder the mysteries of God, I hope you will go ask your own pastor any further questions you have. May God bless your study of His Word, and may He continue to send us faithful pastors to teach us about His love to us in Jesus.

SESSION ONE: MARIANNE

1. Answers will vary.

2. **Pastor McGuire:** No, God's love is not based on our worthiness. God's love is based on the worthiness of Christ who, in turn, makes us worthy. God Himself tells us in His Word that He loves us for Christ's sake. In John 3:16, God is the actor, and we are the recipients. Our worthiness is based on what He's done in giving His Son up into death on the cross.
   Pastor Schuermann: God's love is not based on our worthiness but on His very nature. John writes, "God is love. In this the love of God was made manifest among us, that God sent His only Son into the world, so that we might live through Him. In this is love, not that we have loved God but that He loved us and sent His Son to be the propitiation for our sins" (1 John 4:8–10). He loves us as His creation through Jesus, regardless of any worthiness in us.

3. **Pastor McGuire:** We see God's love most clearly displayed on the cross. There He is, shedding His blood while we were yet sinners and then ascending to be at the right hand of God to intercede for us continually. God doesn't stop there. His love is also there for us in Baptism, in the preached Word, and in the Supper.
   Pastor Schuermann: God chiefly shows us His love by giving us His Son to die on the cross and save us from our sins, but He also shows us His love by providing for us and giving us our daily bread.

4. **Pastor McGuire:** God never withholds His love from us. He says in His Word that nothing can separate us from the love of Jesus. No one is able to pluck us out of His hand. God does give us the terrible capacity to reject Him, which means we can turn our back on His love which is already there.

   Pastor Schuermann: God never withholds His love from us. We have innumerable promises in Scripture of God's care for His people, and He promises never to leave us nor forsake us.

5. **Pastor McGuire:** Forgiveness is a concrete manifestation of love. In John 3:16, we see that God's love for us is manifested in Him sacrificing His Son to forgive us of our sins.

   Pastor Schuermann: Peter writes in 1 Peter 4:8 that "love covers a multitude of sins." In this, we see that the greatest illustration of love is God forgiving us our sins in Christ.

6. **Pastor McGuire:** No, forgiveness is more than a feeling. It is concrete. It is a relationship we have that is based on an event, namely, the cross and the resurrection. Forgiveness is the status between us when we are reconciled to each other, whether we feel that way or not.

   Pastor Schuermann: In forgiving someone, our attitude toward that person may change, but Christian forgiveness is not motivated by what we feel. It is motivated by what we know, namely, that God has forgiven us. Being forgiven by God, we, then, can forgive others regardless of our feelings.

7. **Pastor McGuire:** We can trust that God forgives us, because God Himself says so in His Word. God even knows that in our weakness we need His assurance, so He comes to us again and again in His Word and in His Supper to shore up our assurance that we are forgiven by Him.

   Pastor Schuermann: When it comes to forgiveness, it doesn't matter how we feel about ourselves. The only thing that matters is what God promises to us in His Word, and He promises that our sins are forgiven. Consequently, by forgiving us our sins, God makes us worthy to be receivers of His gifts.

8. **Pastor McGuire:** In order to forgive those who have hurt us the most, we have to start with Christ. No other foundation can be laid. If we go back to what Christ has done for us and realize our lack of worthiness in deserving the lengths to which He went to forgive us, that makes it possible for us to do the same. The fruit that naturally flows out of what God has done for us is our forgiving one another. Since we are reconciled to God through Jesus, we can be reconciled one unto another.

   Pastor Schuermann: It isn't always an easy thing to forgive others. The best thing to do is to recognize that we can't forgive others in and of ourselves. We need God's help to do this. For this reason, we should come to the Lord constantly in prayer, asking Him to give us His Spirit that we might be able to forgive others.

SESSION TWO: CLAIRE

1. Answers will vary.

2. **Pastor McGuire:** To wait on the Lord is to recognize the Lord is your only strength. It is the belief that if help is going to come, it is only going to come through Him. Waiting is itself a picture of faith. If we didn't trust the Lord, we wouldn't wait for Him. **Pastor Schuermann:** God's timing is not always our timing. Waiting on the Lord means trusting that He is still caring for us and watching over us even as we are waiting for our suffering to come to an end. When we wait on the Lord, we trust that He will or will not remove that suffering from us at the proper time.

3. **Pastor McGuire:** For those who wait on Him, God promises victory over anything and everything that would separate us from Him. God promises us life with Him, a life that begins even now on this earth and continues on into life immortal. He promises paradise restored so that the brokenness we feel in this life won't be forever. Christ's miracles on this earth were a preview of what waits in store for those who are in Him.

Pastor Schuermann: God promises for those who wait on Him that His will *will* be done for them. He promises that everything will be okay in the end, though He doesn't necessarily tell us how. He does not promise specific resolutions to specific problems in this life, but He does promise that there will be no suffering in the new, resurrected creation. The fallen world will be gone and everything will be made new and perfect.

4. **Pastor McGuire:** As baptized Christians, the devil has no power over us. Our Baptism is our greatest weapon against the devil, because, in our Baptism, we find our identity: an identity grounded in Christ and in what He has done. Since none of what Christ has done can be undone, our identity in Him is sure. The devil can't change our identity.
Pastor Schuermann: Wherever God is, the devil cannot be. God's name and Spirit were put upon us in our Baptism, so the devil no longer has any power over us. He may tempt us, lie to us, and pretend to have power, but he has none.

5. **Pastor McGuire:** Our greatest resistance against the devil is the Word of God and prayer. The Word of God is sure and infallible. It is the very Word that Christ used in His one-on-one with the devil. Prayer has the promises of God attached to it. In prayer, we get to lay before God our needs and ring into His ears the promises He has made to us. Prayer is not so much about getting God to do something, as much as it is a gift from God to us. Prayer flows out of faith, and, because Christian prayer flows from God's promises to us, the very promises that strengthen our faith are being reinforced.

Pastor Schuermann: The Word of God is our greatest resistance against the devil. It is God's gift to us that we have His Word to listen to, meditate on, and pray back to Him. All of these things destroy the devil, for the Word made flesh has defeated him.

6. **Pastor McGuire:** Luther doesn't have one particular word in mind, but rather the Gospel Word of God: "Jesus loves me; for God so love the world that He gave His only Son; I am baptized into that Son." It is seemingly a light thing. These are just words, yet this Word has the power to crush Satan himself.
   Pastor Schuermann: The one Word that Luther refers to is the name of our Lord Jesus, the Son whose task it was to become incarnate and defeat sin, death, and devil through His work on the cross.

7. **Pastor McGuire:** In our suffering, God promises us certain, sure things: we will be raised from the dead; our bodies will live forever; God will wipe away every tear; He won't distance Himself in our suffering; He affirms our suffering and promises to one day take it away. In fact, it is no small thing amidst suffering to be reminded that our Lord Himself is no stranger to suffering. In a real sense, He suffers with us and He suffers for us. We can approach Him in our prayers knowing that He knows what we are going through. What comfort it is to know that He alone is the only One who has suffered true abandonment by the Father. We never have to experience that. Christ took that upon Himself, so that we can know that we are never truly alone. He is always with us, and He will never forsake us.

Pastor Schuermann: The greatest temptation when we suffer is to believe that God does not care for us and that He has abandoned us; yet, God's Word tells us that He does care for us and that He will never leave us nor forsake us. Christ suffered God's punishment for our sins, so we, the baptized, do not suffer at the hand of God for our sins today. Christ already took on that suffering for us.

8. **Pastor McGuire:** We are never nearer to God than when we are at our lowest. Depression can be a blessing in that it drives us to recognize that His grace is, indeed, sufficient for us (2 Corinthians 12:9).

   Pastor Schuermann: Suffering never feels like a blessing, but it is in the sense that God permits these things to occur in the lives of His children that we might all the more look to Him for all good. As a doctor faithfully cares for his sick patient, the patient learns to trust the care of her doctor. In the same way, God uses our suffering to give us the opportunity to seek His medicine, namely, the Word preached and the body and blood distributed for the forgiveness which heals us.

SESSION THREE: JULIA

1. **Pastor McGuire:** Absolutely not. God helps only those who can't help themselves.
   Pastor Schuermann: This saying is a total lie, and it should be stricken from everyone's vocabulary. God helps those who are the most helpless, chiefly us.

2. **Pastor McGuire:** God's help is not dependent on anything we think, say, or do. Jesus stilling the storm is a perfect example. The disciples were without faith, doubting their Master's care, and Jesus stills the storm anyway.
   Pastor Schuermann: Our acts of obedience have nothing to do with earning God's provision. Our faith, instead, sees that the help God provides for us is a gift. We, like Abraham and Isaac in the wilderness, trust that God will provide the lamb for our sacrifice. We cannot provide our own.

3. **Pastor McGuire:** God sends the rain on the believers and the unbelievers alike (Matthew 5:45).
   Pastor Schuermann: Look at how Jesus talks about God taking care of His creation. He makes the rain fall on the just and the unjust. In this world, we sometimes see the unbelievers prospering more than the believers, and this may come about because the unbelievers have helped and serve themselves. Yet, we as believers know that all things are a gift from God who cares for all of us, His whole creation.

4. **Pastor McGuire:** No, worrying does not add one cubit to our stature.

Pastor Schuermann: Worrying is a form of unbelief. It denies God, refusing to trust that God's promises apply even to us. When we worry, we attempt to take the reins of life in our own hands and put ourselves in control; yet, we do not have it, and worrying will lead us directly to our own helplessness and cause us to despair.

5. **Pastor McGuire:** We cast our anxieties on the Lord by taking them to Him in prayer and trusting that He bears them for us.
   Pastor Schuermann: Tell God what the problem is. He is our Father. He loves us; He listens to us; He rejoices in the trust that leads us to come to Him in prayer. Pray and trust that God is our father and will answer those prayers in the way He thinks is best.

6. **Pastor McGuire:** Seeking first the kingdom of God and His righteousness is finding in Christ the answer to our biggest questions. Does God love me? Where am I going when I die? Where do I stand eternally? With those questions answered in Christ, the temporal questions are kept in perspective.
   Pastor Schuermann: First of all, the righteousness of God is Christ Jesus, and the kingdom of God is Christ's reign inaugurated on the cross. How do we seek these things? We come to wherever Jesus is, to wherever He has promised to be; we listen to the preacher who tells us His Word and go to the table to receive His body and blood; we seek out other Christians who will remind us that we are members of the family of God, made righteous in Christ.

7. **Pastor McGuire:** In giving us the petition "give us this day our daily bread" in the Lord's Prayer, God is showing that this is what He desires and intends to give us.

   Pastor Schuermann: God doesn't lie, and He tells us clearly in His Word that He provides for us.

8. Answers will vary.

SESSION FOUR: FAYE

1. Answers will vary.

2. **Pastor McGuire:** In Romans 8, God promises to make all things new and to restore things to their original goodness. Today, because of our fall into sin, things on this earth decay and die; however, through Christ, God has begun the process of making things new and will consummate them in the resurrection.
Pastor Schuermann: Diseases are symptoms of death. The promise of God is that He will restore us when we are resurrected. All disease will be gone from our glorified bodies.

3. **Pastor McGuire:** From the beginning, God promised to send the Savior, and in that Savior, all generations have access to the Father and the promise of creation restored.
Pastor Schuermann: God promised Abraham that a great nation would come from him and that all people would be blessed through him. The psalmist is looking back and seeing all that God has done to preserve His people and to keep His promises to Abraham. Since God has kept His promises to Israel, the psalmist can look forward and trust that God will continue to keep His promises. We, too, can look back and see God's faithfulness in keeping His promises to Abraham, Israel, and even us. Through the incarnation, death, and resurrection of Jesus, God has blessed us even unto eternal life.

4. **Pastor McGuire:** God's love for us in Christ lasts forever. Jesus lasts forever, and, since we are in Him, we last forever too. We know this to be true from God's external Word which made us alive in Christ at our Baptism and continues to strengthen and preserve us in the eating and drinking of the Lord's Supper.
   Pastor Schuermann: Christ is the same yesterday, today, and forever. He lasts forever, and so do His promises. Having been baptized into His name, we now last forever too. We know this because God says so in His Word.

5. **Pastor McGuire:** Our identity in Christ is the most important thing in the life of every Christian because it never fades away. We can never lose it because it is based on God's Word and God's work in Christ Jesus, who is the same yesterday, today, and forever.
   Pastor Schuermann: Faye's Baptism, where Christ washed her from sin and clothed her with His robes, is most important. Baptism, where God visibly acts to make us new and gives us Christ, is God's gift to all of us. God brings us into His kingdom in Baptism, branding us with His name and claiming us as His child. It is all God's action, so we can't lose it. We can never be snatched away from God's hand. We can walk away from it, but we can't lose it.

6. **Pastor McGuire:** The First Commandment helps refocus our lives on what is most important by centering our lives on the life of the One who gave us and redeemed our life.
   Pastor Schuermann: The First Commandment tells us what is most important: that we should fear, love, and trust in God above all things.

7. **Pastor McGuire:** We can be faithful friends to our brothers and sisters in Christ who are suffering from loss by being present in their lives. We can visit them as Christ has visited us and encouraged us to do in the parable of the sheep and the goats: "'I was sick and you visited me, I was in prison and you came to me'" (Matthew 25:36). It's being Christlike to be present for the other.

   Pastor Schuermann: We can be faithful friends to the family of God in times of loss by sticking to God's promises. Don't make up things that you think might make people feel better. Our words have no weight behind them, but God's Word is everything. Consequently, we can also listen to God's desires for us by serving our neighbor, taking care of her, showing mercy to her, and helping her in her time of need.

8. Answers will vary, but Pastor Schuermann recommends memorizing "Lord, Thee I Love with All My Heart" (*LSB* 708).

SESSION FIVE: EMILY

1. **Pastor McGuire:** Righteousness is doing the things you ought to do.
   Pastor Schuermann: Righteousness is a clear conscience before God.

2. **Pastor McGuire:** We cannot become righteous through keeping the Law because we are naturally born sinners. Scripture tells us that we are not only incapable of keeping the Law but that we desire to break it. We're opposed to God. We are enemies of Him.
   Pastor Schuermann: As soon as we break one commandment, we have failed to keep them all. As soon as we break a law, our conscience and, subsequently, our righteousness is toast.

3. **Pastor McGuire:** We become righteous by faith in Christ.
   Pastor Schuermann: We become righteous through Christ in Baptism. It is there that God gives us a clean conscience. As Peter writes, "For Christ also suffered once for sins, the righteous for the unrighteous, that He might bring us to God, being put to death in the flesh but made alive in the spirit, . . . Baptism, which corresponds to this, now saves you, not as a removal of dirt from the body but as an appeal to God for a good conscience, through the resurrection of Jesus Christ" (1 Peter 3:18, 21).

4. **Pastor McGuire:** The righteousness based on faith of which Paul writes in his epistle to the Romans is Christ's righteousness which is freely credited to us and received by faith.

   Pastor Schuermann: If we are given a clean conscience before God in Christ, then the righteousness based on faith is one that believes Christ's righteousness is ours. We trust that Christ's righteousness has been given to us by God.

5. **Pastor McGuire:** The Law is that Word of God which commands us, threatens us, and ultimately shows us our sin. It instructs us in our actions, our thoughts, and our deeds and tells us what they should be in order to please God. The Gospel is the free gift of forgiveness won for us by Jesus on the cross. It is the message that God has done that which we were unable to do. The Law is never the basis for our salvation, only the Gospel is. We want to keep the two as far away from each other as we can when it comes to understanding our salvation.

   Pastor Schuermann: The Law is what God demands. The Law says, "Do." The Gospel is what God has done for us. The Gospel says, "Done." In relationship to the Law, the Gospel is the truth that the Law has been fulfilled in Christ. As we read God's Word, we always need to be thinking about who is being expected to do the action and who is acting. If we are expected to do the action, then it is Law. If we are the recipients of God's action, then it is Gospel.

6. **Pastor McGuire:** It is important to always put God in the subject whenever we talk about salvation and our life in the Church because God is our only hope. There is no other name known by man under which one can be saved. Christ's atoning sacrifice on the cross is all-sufficient. As Paul writes in his epistle, "It is no longer I who live, but Christ who lives in me" (Galatians 2:20).

   Pastor Schuermann: If we put ourselves in the subject doing the action, then we are putting ourselves in charge of our own salvation. We do not want to do that because it will not end well.

7. **Pastor McGuire:** It is tempting to put ourselves in the subject and focus on what we do for God because that sinful nature with which we are all born always turns us in on ourselves. Instead, by being the object of what God has done, we find our salvation secure. We could never be that secure if we were the subject.

   Pastor Schuermann: Our old Adam wants to stand before God and man and say, "Hey, look at me!" The old Adam takes the good works that God has prepared for us to do through the working of the Holy Spirit and tries to claim them for himself, for his own merit. That is sin. That is why we are tempted to put ourselves in the subject doing the action; however, we are recipients of God's good work in Jesus. When God does something, He does it perfectly. Who doesn't want that? To be the beneficiary of such work is an honor and a privilege.

8. **Pastor McGuire:** Instead of focusing on our own good works, we should focus on God's good work for us, His gifts to us (Baptism and the Lord's Supper), and the benefits of His gifts.

Pastor Schuermann: If we focus on what we do, we will always be left with the doubt of whether or not we are doing enough or are loving God enough. If we instead focus on what God is doing for us, we know it is enough because He says it is: "My grace is sufficient for you" (2 Corinthians 12:9). Where can we go today to find God doing something for us? On Sunday morning when we come to church, Christ is present. He preaches to us from His Word; He feeds us His body and blood; and, if there is a Baptism, we see Him making a sinful being a child of God. In church, we have the chief gifts of God where we might come again and again to receive them.

SESSION SIX: ANNA

1. **Pastor McGuire:** The hole in each of our hearts is the sin which we have inherited from our first parents, Adam and Eve. Christ came to heal us and make us whole. He did this on the cross when He, in our place, died for our sins so that we might have forgiveness and that our hole might be patched.
   Pastor Schuermann: We are lost and condemned creatures, born astray from God. The hole in our heart is sin, and God's medicine of forgiveness heals it. Put another way, the hole is our mortality, our death in sin, and God heals the hole by giving us immortality through His life-giving Word.

2. **Pastor McGuire:** God tells us in His Word that He neither slumbers nor sleeps. He watches over us, and our care of our children reflects that.
   Pastor Schuermann: The Scriptures reveal God as long suffering. He puts up with a whole lot of sin, rejection, and grief from His people. Even through all of this, He always has in mind His eternal promise of salvation in Christ.

3. **Pastor McGuire:** God provides for us by giving us health, food, shelter, jobs, family, friends, good government, and every good and perfect thing.
   Pastor Schuermann: God provides us with all that we need to support this body and life.

4. **Pastor McGuire:** God sustains and preserves our lives through means. For our temporal needs, He cares for us through vocation, or through human channels. We are each masks of God's providence, caring for one another through our work as doctors, nurses, loving parents, caring friends, and so many more. God also provides for our spiritual needs through means, delivering the forgiveness of sins to us through the Word in Baptism and the Lord's Supper.

   Pastor Schuermann: God provides all the things we need to support this body and life, but He also provides us with so much more. He not only takes care of our temporal needs but also our eternal needs. He provides us with a sure and certain hope that we are forgiven and have eternal life in Christ.

5. **Pastor McGuire:** In praying the petition "Give us this day our daily bread," we are asking God for those things we need to support this body and life. At the same time, in praying this petition, we are acknowledging Him as the giver of these things and giving Him thanks for it.

   Pastor Schuermann: We are asking God to do what He promises to do and already does, namely, to take care of us, provide for us, and give us everything we need.

6. **Pastor McGuire:** The Church is a mask of God, channeling His provision to the people. The Church is to reflect God's love in its care of the less fortunate and should always be about providing for the unemployed, the homeless, the orphans, the widows, and generally making sure no one is deprived of those means of sustenance.

Pastor Schuermann: God calls us to show mercy to our neighbor in need, and that can be done in a multitude of ways. Jesus bids us to feed the hungry, clothe the poor, visit those who are in prison, and tend to the sick. Even beyond that, He bids us to be there with His message of forgiveness and love for them in Christ.

7. **Pastor McGuire:** God's promise to neither slumber nor sleep should let us know that He is there and has our best interest at heart, even when all evidence is seemingly contrary.
   Pastor Schuermann: "The LORD is my light and my salvation; whom shall I fear? The LORD is the stronghold of my life; of whom shall I be afraid?" (Psalm 27:1). God's never-failing presence for us is so different from what we experience from our earthly neighbors because God is always tending to us and caring for us without ceasing. Sometimes, He does this through our neighbors, but we can recognize that it is God caring for us through them.

8. The point made is an instruction rather than a question.

SESSION SEVEN: DIEDRE

1. **Pastor McGuire:** Love is a concrete action of kindness and mercy directed toward another and oriented toward the other's well-being. Everything about love is outward looking. In Scripture, love is a matter of doing. We see love's action most clearly in God sending His Son and giving Him up on the cross. We don't know love apart from this action. Love is not solely an attitude or a feeling; love is not self-gratification; love is not doing something for the sake of self but, instead, for the sake of the other. The apostles exhort us in Scripture to love others, and that makes no sense if love is only a feeling. It only makes sense if the apostles have in mind an action toward someone outside of yourself. Paul says that whether you feel loving toward someone or not, here's what you do: you love them. Paul has in mind not a feeling but an action toward someone outside of yourself.

   Pastor Schuermann: There are different words for love in the Greek. In 1 Corinthians 13, *agape* is the word for love that is used. *Agape* is the love that shows itself in service to the neighbor. This *agape* is most perfectly expressed in Jesus, for it is the same love that God shows us in John 3:16. Our own *agape* is seen in the act of serving and caring for others. Love, in the truest sense of the word, is never really an emotion. It is a relationship word, not a description of one's feelings.

2. **Pastor McGuire** and **Pastor Schuermann:** Love helps our neighbor.

3. **Pastor McGuire:** Faith is strengthened only by the Word, and that Word teaches us the lengths to which Christ went for us. Our own acts of giving care help give us a glimpse into the care God exercises on our behalf.
Pastor Schuermann: We know our faith is fed and strengthened by the Holy Spirit, so we seek out wherever the Holy Spirit might be. In God's Word, we are promised that the Holy Spirit is present wherever the Word is proclaimed, the Sacraments are distributed, and the people of God are gathered in His name. That is where faith is strengthened.

4. **Pastor McGuire:** Our neighbor is anyone God has put in our life.
Pastor Schuermann: The best way to find your neighbor is to look around and ask two questions: "Where am I? Who is with me?" That's your neighbor.

5. Answers will vary.

6. **Pastor McGuire:** In such a case, it is important that the caregiver at least talk to her pastor. We don't always know when it is time to let go and seek help in giving care, so it is helpful to have another person's objective opinion from outside of us say whether or not it is time or, instead, that we are copping out too soon. It is helpful to remember that caregiving is about serving another, not about whether or not giving care is standing in the way of the kind of life we want to live. The better question to ask when considering whether or not to let go and seek help giving care is, "Is the kind of care I am able to give actually able to help this person or not?" Even when you ask yourself this question, it is still best to have someone else help you make the decision.

Pastor Schuermann: The best way to know if we should seek help in giving care to our neighbor is if the care we are able to give is not enough to meet our neighbor's needs. It can be a hard thing to face this realization, especially if our neighbor is someone we love; however, if we can no longer care for our neighbor in the way that she needs—provide a safe environment, maintain her health, etc.—it is good and right to seek further help. In fact, it is serving your neighbor to do so.

7. **Pastor McGuire:** We can be supportive and loving to the caregiver God gives us by not demanding more than we need. Also, we can do away with our pride and not refuse the care our caregiver has to give.

Pastor Schuermann: It is always helpful to recognize who your caregiver is: Christ's gift to you to take care of you, to help you, and to serve you. You should, then, regard and treat your caregiver as such a gift. Pray for her, listen to her, trust her, and thank her. Cheerfully live out your vocation as the one being cared for and know that it is good.

8. **Pastor McGuire:** Love never ends because we will always have neighbors to love. In heaven, there is no longer any need for faith because we will finally see face-to-face the One in whom we have believed. There is also no need for hope in heaven because our hope will have been fulfilled; however, we will continue to love our fellow saints.
Pastor Schuermann: As John writes, "God is love" (1 John 4:8). Love finds its source in God. Since God's love for us does not end, neither does our love for our neighbor.

SESSION EIGHT: LAURA

1. **Pastor McGuire:** No, Garret is alive. As Paul says, to live is Christ and to die is gain. Whether we live or die, we are always Christ's.
Pastor Schuermann: As Paul writes, "We know that Christ, being raised from the dead, will never die again; death no longer has dominion over Him" (Romans 6:9). Since Garret is baptized into Christ and forgiven in Christ, death no longer has dominion over him either. He, with Christ, is alive.

2. **Pastor McGuire:** We died in our Baptism.
Pastor Schuermann: We died to sin at the font when Christ's death to sin was applied to us. We do die physically at a certain point in time, but that death is temporary. We know that Christ died at a certain point in time as well, but He was then raised again from the dead. That promise of resurrection is for us in Christ as well.

3. **Pastor McGuire:** Now that we have died with Christ in our Baptism, our hope is that we will rise with Him. Even now, we are raised to newness of life. Eternity has already started for us.
Pastor Schuermann: We not only have Christ's death in our Baptism, but we also have Christ's resurrection. Death no longer has dominion over us. We will be raised from the dead too.

4. **Pastor McGuire:** We still sin because the old self is still there. He won't be gotten rid of until our Last Day.

Pastor Schuermann: As Paul writes, "For I have the desire to do what is right, but not the ability to carry it out. For I do not do the good I want, but the evil I do not want is what I keep on doing" (Romans 7:18–19). We have both an old man, Adam, and new man, Christ, in us. That old, sinful Adam was drowned in our Baptism, but, as Luther puts it, he is a really good swimmer. He will finally be put to death in our flesh with our bodily death. In the meantime, we still struggle against him in our sinful flesh.

5. **Pastor McGuire:** Our own flesh still perishes and dies because our flesh is still subject to the curse on sin. God chooses not to destroy our flesh and start again from nothing, but, instead, to remake and transform our old flesh in the same way He did with Christ Himself. We will not rise with a different flesh but with the same flesh now glorified.
   Pastor Schuermann: It is a mystery as to why God doesn't just make everything perfect immediately, but, in His wisdom, He doesn't. We continue to sin as well as cry out with Paul, "Who will deliver me from this body of death?" (Romans 7:24). When we die, it is to put that sinful flesh to death, that we would be raised to eternal life in Christ on the Last Day.

6. **Pastor McGuire:** This petition means that one day the dead in Christ will rise again in their bodies. It is a full-bodied salvation that God gives us. Our bodies will be raised but made new to live forever in Christ's presence.

Pastor Schuermann: On the Last Day, Christ will return and call all the dead from their graves, giving new life to all who have died in Christ. Sin being absent, there will be no more death.

7. **Pastor McGuire:** Laura can be thankful that God kept the promise He made her son in his Baptism, and he is even now in the arms of the Savior awaiting the resurrection.

   Pastor Schuermann: Laura can be thankful that God gave her the gift of a son; that her son, in life on this earth, faithfully served his neighbor as a soldier, an honorable, God-pleasing vocation; and that God loved her son so much that He gave him the gift of the forgiveness of his sins and salvation in his Baptism. Her son died in Christ, so he lives.

8. **Pastor McGuire:** Our hope and comfort in the face of death is that we will rise again. The Lord is risen, indeed! Alleluia!

   Pastor Schuermann: We really have only one true hope and comfort in the face of death: the promise that Christ has paid for our sin and that He will raise us up on the Last Day to be with Him forever.

SESSION NINE: HOPE

1. **Pastor McGuire:** We have in the Holy Spirit an intercessor who prays for us when we are unable to pray for ourselves.
   Pastor Schuermann: God knows everything, even what we need. Jesus says during His Sermon on the Mount, "Your Father knows what you need before you ask Him" (Matthew 6:8). God knows what we need even without our prayers. Also, prayer does not require us to speak audibly. God knows the desires of our heart, and He promises that the Spirit will intercede for us, bringing our petitions before God without us saying anything.

2. **Pastor McGuire:** Yes, God always answers our prayers.
   Pastor Schuermann: Jesus says, "For everyone who asks receives, and the one who seeks finds, and to the one who knocks it will be opened" (Matthew 7:8). In this passage, Jesus is talking about prayer. Here is a promise from our Lord that our prayer is answered. There is no promise that it will be answered the way we want, just that it will be answered.

3. **Pastor McGuire:** God will not always give us everything we want because the "good thing" referred to by the psalmist is up to God. Faith trusts that God has our best interest at heart, and that may not always coincide with what we want.

Pastor Schuermann: Nowhere does the psalmist say that those who seek the Lord get what they want. He says that we lack no good thing. Paul asked the Lord three times to remove his thorn in the flesh, yet the Lord did not take it away. If Paul doesn't always get exactly what he wants from Lord, we should not expect to either. We will, however, always get what we need from God.

4. **Pastor McGuire:** God promises to answer the prayer of the righteous. He will bear their afflictions and be with them in all circumstances.
   Pastor Schuermann: God promises the righteous that He hears their prayers, answers their prayers, and cares and provides for them as a father does for his dear children.

5. **Pastor McGuire:** We should pray always through Christ for He is the One who gives us access to the throne of God in the first place. We also should pray as Jesus did, according to God's will.
   Pastor Schuermann: When the disciples asked Jesus how they should pray, He gave them the Lord's Prayer. That is a good start for us as well. In reality, that prayer covers just about everything, but we do not have to stop there. We can come to the Lord with anything and tell Him what we need, trusting that He hears us.

6. **Pastor McGuire:** You can say the Lord's Prayer clearly and boldly during the Divine Service as well as encourage parents to pray the Lord's Prayer every day with their children, whether in the morning, before a meal, or at bedtime.

Pastor Schuermann: Say the Lord's Prayer slowly. Do no rush through it in the service. Work with the children, encouraging them and teaching them, whether in Sunday School or at home.

7. **Pastor McGuire:** We absolutely have the opportunity to taste and see that the Lord is good in the Lord's Supper as well as in every gift that He gives us, including Baptism and the hearing of His Word. In every gift He gives, we can see it through the eyes of the One who was given us His name in Baptism. The First Article gifts start with the words, "I believe." That's what separates us from the pagan. In faith, we can see all things in creation as good gifts from a good giver. The pagan can't do that.

   Pastor Schuermann: Most obviously, we can taste and see that the Lord is good in the Service of the Sacrament when we come to the altar to partake of our Lord's body and blood. Also, there are plenty of times in Scripture when God's Word is described as a feast. We can know that when we hear God's Word and believe what we hear, we are hearing, tasting, and seeing how good the Lord is.

8. **Pastor McGuire:** We can help everyone in the Church receive Christ's good gifts by doing everything we can to overcome the barrier that their disability presents, to communicate Christ's gifts to them in their particular heart language, and to bring the Gospel to them in the form in which they can receive it.

Pastor Schuermann: Make sure your church service is communicating in a way that all can understand. If you have deaf members, have someone sign the service or provide a written copy of the service and sermon to them; if blind, make a braille *Lutheran Service Book* available to them; if mute, encourage them and reassure them that their prayers and praises are just as valid before God whether spoken aloud or not in the service; if lame, reassure them that they do not need to stand during the service but that you can come to them with Holy Communion. Whoever our brothers and sisters in Christ are and whatever needs they may have, we should go up to them, greet them, share the peace of the Lord with them, and treat each of them as an equal member of the Body of Christ, building them up in the faith.

1. **Pastor McGuire:** The psalmist tells us that children are a blessing. When the psalmist uses the word *blessing*, he is describing an objective condition. To be blessed by the Lord is to be in His favor, so, in Psalm 127, children represent a sign of divine favor.
   Pastor Schuermann: Children are not ours. They are a gift we receive from God's hand. The Lord calls the man who has children blessed.

2. **Pastor McGuire:** Yes, God wills for children to be the good fruit of the one-flesh union in marriage.
   Pastor Schuermann: Twice in God's Word, He bids His creation to be fruitful and multiply: once, to Adam and Eve, and second, to Noah and his family after the flood. Children are a part of marriage. When God brings a man and a woman together and joins them as one flesh, children are the intended fruit of that union.

3. **Pastor McGuire:** We grow accustomed to a certain lifestyle. We treasure our trips to Napa Valley, our free time, our conveniences, our quiet, and our freedom to go where we want to go when we want to go. Children stand in the way of all of those things, yet a Christian should not intentionally take steps to avoid conception. Because God calls children a blessing, we cannot see them as anything but that. (If a doctor makes the case that a pregnancy could kill the wife or if a spouse wants to avoid transmitting a venereal disease, in both circumstances one could take steps to preserve the life of the spouse; however, spouses should not specifically avoid the gift of children.)

Pastor Schuermann: The world tempts us not to have children. It bids us to be successful, to achieve certain worldly goals, and to fulfill certain plans in life. Often times, these goals and plans are pitted against marriage and children. We also tempt ourselves not to have children because we are selfish. Having children is a lot of work, and we don't want to do that work; having children can be expensive, and we want to have that money for ourselves; and having children requires tremendous self-sacrifice, and we don't want to give up our time, our careers, our possessions, and our desirous plans. In regards to whether or not it is ever okay to avoid the gift of children, it is important to ask yourself if you are avoiding them because you don't want them. If that is the case, then there is a spiritual problem that needs to be worked through. There can be specific medical circumstances where the health and even the very life of a parent might be jeopardized by carrying a pregnancy, but most people don't encounter these circumstances in their lives. Couples should discuss such difficult decisions with their doctor and their pastor..

4. **Pastor McGuire:** As with other aspects of a fallen creation that groans under the curse God placed on it with the first sin, the lack of children in a marriage is not a specific judgment by God against that couple. It is simply one of the unfortunate manifestations of a world not yet remade.

Pastor Schuermann: We cannot ultimately say for what reasons God might be withholding the gift of children from a particular married couple, but we can say that it is most definitely not because God is punishing them for their personal sins. The punishment for our individual sins was already laid upon Jesus on the cross. We do, however, live in a fallen world. Adam and Eve subjected all of the world to sin, and the world is now broken. Barrenness is a manifestation of that brokenness.

5. **Pastor McGuire:** Mary teaches us to receive God's gifts in faith.
   Pastor Schuermann: If we look at Mary's circumstances, there is very little good going for her at this moment. She is engaged to be married and has just been told that she is pregnant with the Messiah. She is going to have cultural ramifications to face with this news, and her faithful response is to let it be as God wills. We can learn from her faithful example that what we receive from God is good for us, and we can rejoice in His will and trust that it is good.

6. **Pastor McGuire:** The promise from God to always provide for His children comes in the Lord's Prayer itself: "Give us this day our daily bread." We can have every confidence that God will provide us with the bread that we and our children need to live.
   Pastor Schuermann: God will always provide the means because He gives us our daily bread. If we acknowledge what God's Word says to be true, namely, that children are a gift from Him, then we can trust that He will also provide a way for us to care for those children.

7. **Pastor McGuire:** Our specific responsibilities in rearing the children God has given to us are bringing them to the saving waters of Baptism, raising them in the knowledge and nurture of their Lord Jesus, providing for them physically, and teaching them the will of God. People who have not been given the gift of children can be parents in the Church by helping watch and care for children during the Divine Service, teaching Sunday School, modeling the faith for them, and offering care to help give their parents a break.

Pastor Schuermann: First and foremost, God's expectation of us is to raise our children in the fear and knowledge of Him; to bring them to the font to be baptized; to bring them to the Word to hear it; to teach them of Jesus and His salvation for them; and to teach them to pray. God also expects parents to care for the bodily needs of their children, and He promises to provide the means to do that. Those who have not been given children of their own can help serve and care for the children in their church through many different vocations: Sunday School teachers, VBS volunteers, youth group leaders, choir directors, babysitters, song leaders, and godparents. These people can pray for the children in their congregation and help the parents in raising them in the Church. Baptized children are just as much members of the Body of Christ as adults, so we should treat them as such.

8. **Pastor McGuire:** Baptism is the equivalent of Jesus taking the children in His arms and blessing them. We should then, first and foremost, bring the children to Baptism. After that, we should continue bringing the children to church for the Divine Service and teaching them the Scriptures at home.

   Pastor Schuermann: Along with the instruction to let the little children come to Him, God includes a warning: Do not hinder them. We, therefore, should not withhold our children from the saving waters of Baptism, but bring them to be baptized, speak the Word to them, pray for them, and help them to be in the Divine Service by encouraging parents to bring them to church.

SESSION ELEVEN: CHRISTINE

1. Answers will vary.

2. **Pastor McGuire:** God does not punish you for your personal sins because the punishment has already been borne by Christ in your place.
   Pastor Schuermann: God's punishment was laid upon Jesus. Whatever individual sins you may commit (which do deserve punishment), Jesus suffered the punishment for those sins in your place. As Isaiah writes, "the LORD has laid on Him the iniquity of us all" (Isaiah 53:6).

3. **Pastor McGuire:** You can know with certainty that you are a child of God because you are baptized. As His heir, God promises to give you His continual, gracious presence, the promise of health irreversibly perfected on the day of resurrection, and eternal life with God in the new heaven and the new earth.
   Pastor Schuermann: In John 3, Jesus talks about how one will enter the kingdom of God, and He says that one must be born again of water and the Spirit. Jesus is talking about Baptism where we are born into God's family. In Baptism, we have full confidence and assurance that we are God's children and that He is our Father. As our Father, God promises that we will receive the inheritance of sons, namely, salvation from our sin which was earned by Jesus, the only begotten Son of God.

4. **Pastor McGuire:** None of us is good. Faith in Christ is what makes us good in the eyes of God.
   Pastor Schuermann: As Isaiah writes, all of our deeds are as filthy rags (Isaiah 64:6). We are clothed with Jesus' pure garment in Baptism, so God no longer sees the filthy sinner when He looks at us. He now sees one who has been clothed with Jesus' blood and righteousness.

5. **Pastor McGuire:** Good works do not earn God's favor. We do good works simply out of love for the neighbor who actually needs them. Now that Christ has taken care of our relationship with God, we can freely serve our neighbor without keeping an eye to God to make sure He is watching us.
   Pastor Schuermann: Scripture is clear that we are saved by grace through faith so that no one should boast. God does not need our good works; our neighbor does. Just as we have been served by the Son of Man, so do we serve our neighbor. In fact, God, in His mercy, has prepared good works in advance for us to do so that we might serve our neighbor.

6. **Pastor McGuire:** This saying implies that there are degrees to being a Christian. Either we are good in God's eyes through Christ or not.
   Pastor Schuermann: The Holy Spirit through the Word shows us our sin, so we can see that we are not good because of anything we do. We need something from outside of ourselves to make us good in the eyes of God. We are only good because Jesus has given us His name.

7. **Pastor McGuire:** We can expect to suffer in this life because we are still part of a fallen world, laboring under the curse for sin. God Himself tells us this will be the case until the Last Day. In the face of suffering, however, we have comfort in knowing that God has prepared for those who believe in His Son the end of suffering. In Revelation 7, we have a description of heaven as having no pain.

   Pastor Schuermann: Good works don't earn us anything. We should not think that they have any correlation as to how well our life will go on this earth. The fact is that our Lord tells us that we will have suffering in this life. He doesn't necessarily tell us how much, but we can expect it. The greatest comfort we have in the face of suffering is that the Lord is with us and that He is watching over us, protecting us, and caring for us.

8. **Pastor McGuire:** Even while suffering from cancer, Christine can rejoice that she is God's child. Whether death comes by the means of this cancer or not, she has already died in her Baptism and been made alive in Christ Jesus.

   Pastor Schuermann: Christine's true victory is that her cancer, an agent of death, has no power over her, for death has been defeated by Christ. As Paul says, " 'O death, where is your victory? O death, where is your sting? . . . thanks be to God, who gives us the victory through our Lord Jesus Christ' " (1 Corinthians 15:55, 57).

SESSION TWELVE: EVE

1. Answers will vary.

2. **Pastor McGuire:** We are to cast our worries on the Lord because He cares for us. Our English translations of 1 Peter 5:7 don't do it justice. The word order in the Greek sounds a little clunkier, but the point it makes is even more comforting: "because to Him it belongs concerning you." In other words, Peter is saying to cast your cares on Him because caring for you is His job. The emphasis is on "to Him." To Him belongs the job of caring for your worries, not to you. It is His job, not yours.
   Pastor Schuermann: Our Lord wants us to cast our burdens on Him that He might care for us. As the psalmist writes, "Cast your burden on the LORD, and He will sustain you; He will never permit the righteous to be moved" (Psalm 55:22).

3. **Pastor McGuire:** Take your sleepless hours and redeem them. Get out the Bible and read through a book in the Old or New Testament you haven't read in awhile. Pray. Paul says in Philippians that whatever is true, honorable, just, pure, lovely, and so on, think on these things. Have your Bible and hymnal ready so that when you are weaker and less alert in the waking hours of the night, you can do battle with the demons and the ugly thoughts, worries, and anxieties that plague you.

Pastor Schuermann: We are to bring our cares before the Lord in prayer and clothe ourselves with the armor of His Word. The Word defeats the devil and drives away the demons.

4. **Pastor McGuire:** We can care for our loved ones who are suffering in as many ways as they have temporal needs. Take as your template the words Christ gave in the parable of the sheep and the goats: feed, water, welcome, clothe, and visit His sheep. "Lord, have mercy" is a beautiful prayer because it reminds us of our need for God's mercy. It sums up the attitude we all have toward our gracious Savior: we need His mercy, and He is the gracious mercy-giver. We pray this prayer in confidence that He does give us mercy, not on the basis of our own merit or deserving, but solely out of His gracious love.
   Pastor Schuermann: We can best serve our loved ones who are suffering by praying for them and by just being with them. Listen to them, speak the Word of God to them, and, if you are able, take care of any needs they have. Praying "Lord, have mercy" acknowledges the One who truly is our help: the Lord.

5. **Pastor McGuire:** It is important for a mother of adult children to abide in the Word, so that she can in turn share that Word with her children when they need it. Also, it is important for her to listen to her children.
   Pastor Schuermann: Be present in the lives of those you love. Listen to them, pray for them, and speak the Word of God to them.

6. **Pastor McGuire:** When we serve our neighbor, we do what the neighbor needs, not always what the neighbor wants. It is always right to do that which is in the best interest of our neighbor. This is true also when it comes to taking care of our parents. If Eve is breaking the Fourth Commandment in doing what her parents need done for their own safety and protection, then she should sin boldly.

   Pastor Schuermann: The Fourth Commandment isn't a license for parents to command their children to do only what the parents want. At the same time, it also is not a command for children to do whatever their parents tell them to do. It is a command for children to honor their parents, to recognize them as a mask of the authority of God in their lives, to listen to them, to be obedient to them, to respect them, and to do what is best for them.

7. **Pastor McGuire:** We should not forget that when we care for our aging parents, we are honoring them. Whenever you do something that is in the best interest of your parents, you are honoring them, protecting them, and effectively keeping the Fourth Commandment.

   Pastor Schuermann: We are to pray for them, encourage them, be gentle with them (especially when decisions need to be made about them or for them that may make them uncomfortable), and serve them.

8. **Pastor McGuire:** Take a passage of Scripture or a hymn stanza and work on committing it to memory. One of two things is going to happen. Either you are going to have that much more of the Word in your heart, or you are going to fall asleep, which solves the original problem.

Pastor Schuermann: Use this time to pray. Pull out the Bible and read God's Word. Or, get up and do chores that serve and take care of your spouse or your neighbor that is in need.

THANK YOU TO...

my pew sisters,

> Julie Becker, Courtney Bone, Lucy Brown, Freida Carson, Ann Massey, Margaret Murrell, Pauline Onken, Emily Ottmers, Nancy Van Schaik, Gloria, Cindy, and anonymous contributors. Thank you for sharing your stories of God's faithfulness in your lives with all of us.

my pastors,

> Rev. Brent McGuire and Rev. Michael Schuermann, for answering all of my study questions.

Peggy Kuethe

> for coming up with the brilliant "Moment in the Pew" idea and for being such an encouraging editor.

Dcs. Rose E. Adle

> for being a servant of mercy to all pew sisters and for writing a foreword for this book.

Michael

> for being willing to talk me through any and every theological conundrum.

my mom,

> Cynthia Roley, for being my high school English teacher and my lifelong encourager.

the thesaurus on my Mac

> for keeping my word bank account full.